高等职业教育工程机械类专业规划教材

Professional English of Engineering and Machinery
# 工程机械专业英语

吴明华　陈晓娟　**主　编**
　杨　川　李　活　**副主编**
郁玉叶［安徽农业大学］
连香姣［北京建筑大学］　**主　审**

人民交通出版社股份有限公司
China Communications Press Co.,Ltd.

## 内 容 提 要

本书介绍了柴油发动机、柴油机燃油供给系统、发动机冷却系统和润滑系统、传动系统、发动机起动系统、液压系统、筑路机械、路面养护机械、设备维护、动态仿真技术在工程机械设计上的应用等内容。通过学习,学生可将两到三个学期所涉及的专业基础课和专业核心贯穿起来,并且可以了解专业知识、掌握大量相关的专业英语词汇,为进一步深造打下坚实的基础。

本书可供高等职业院校工程机械类专业师生教学使用。

**图书在版编目(CIP)数据**

工程机械专业英语/吴明华主编. —北京:人民交通出版社股份有限公司,2014.6
高等职业教育工程机械类专业规划教材
ISBN 978-7-114-11407-6

Ⅰ. ①工⋯　Ⅱ. ①吴⋯　Ⅲ. ①工程机械—英语—高等职业教育—教材　Ⅳ. ①H31

中国版本图书馆 CIP 数据核字(2014)第 088851 号

高等职业教育工程机械类专业规划教材

| | |
|---|---|
| 书　名: | 工程机械专业英语 |
| 著 作 者: | 吴明华　陈晓娟 |
| 责任编辑: | 丁润铎　周　凯 |
| 出版发行: | 人民交通出版社股份有限公司 |
| 地　　址: | (100011)北京市朝阳区安定门外外馆斜街3号 |
| 网　　址: | http://www.ccpress.com.cn |
| 销售电话: | (010) 59757973 |
| 总 经 销: | 人民交通出版社股份有限公司发行部 |
| 经　　销: | 各地新华书店 |
| 印　　刷: | 北京市密东印刷有限公司 |
| 开　　本: | 787×1092　1/16 |
| 印　　张: | 7 |
| 字　　数: | 180 千 |
| 版　　次: | 2014年6月　第1版 |
| 印　　次: | 2022年12月　第6次印刷 |
| 书　　号: | ISBN 978-7-114-11407-6 |
| 定　　价: | 20.00 元 |

(有印刷、装订质量问题的图书由本公司负责调换)

# 高等职业教育工程机械类专业
# 规划教材编审委员会

**主 任 委 员** 张　铁(山东交通学院)

**副主任委员**

沈　旭(南京交通职业技术学院)　　　邰　茜(河南交通职业技术学院)
吕其惠(广东交通职业技术学院)　　　吴幼松(安徽交通职业技术学院)
李文耀(山西交通职业技术学院)　　　贺玉斌(内蒙古大学)

**委　　员**

丁成业(南京交通职业技术学院)　　　王　健(内蒙古大学)
王　俊(安徽交通职业技术学院)　　　王德进(新疆交通职业技术学院)
田兴强(贵州交通职业技术学院)　　　代绍军(云南交通职业技术学院)
孙珍娣(新疆交通职业技术学院)　　　闫佐廷(辽宁省交通高等专科学校)
刘　波(辽宁省交通高等专科学校)　　祁贵珍(内蒙古大学)
吴明华(安徽交通职业技术学院)　　　杜艳霞(河南交通职业技术学院)
吴　哲(辽宁省交通高等专科学校)　　陈华卫(四川交通职业技术学院)
李云聪(山西交通职业技术学院)　　　李光林(山东交通职业技术学院)
张炳根(湖南交通职业技术学院)　　　杨　川(成都铁路学校)
杨长征(河南交通职业技术学院)　　　赵　波(辽宁省交通高等专科学校)
高贵宝(山东职业学院)　　　　　　　徐化娟(甘肃交通职业技术学院)
徐永杰(鲁东大学)　　　　　　　　　罗江红(新疆交通职业技术学院)
张宏春(江苏省交通技师学校)　　　　田晓华(江苏省扬州技师学院)

**特邀编审委员**

万汉驰(三一重工股份有限公司)　　　刘士杰(中交西安筑路机械有限公司)
孔渭翔(徐工集团挖掘机械有限公司)　张立银(山推工程机械股份有限公司工程机械研究总院)
王彦章(中国龙工挖掘机事业部)　　　李世坤(中交西安筑路机械有限公司)
王国超(山东临工工程机械有限公司重机公司)　李太杰(西安达刚路面机械股份有限公司)
孔德锋(济南力拓工程机械有限公司)　季旭涛(力士德工程机械股份有限公司)
韦　耿(广西柳工机械股份有限公司挖掘机事业部)　赵家宏(福建晋工机械有限公司)
田志成(国家工程机械质量监督检验中心)　姚录廷(青岛科泰重工机械有限公司)
冯克敏(成都市新筑路桥机械股份有限公司)　顾少航(中联重科股份有限公司渭南分公司)
任华杰(徐工集团筑路机械有限公司)　谢　耘(山东临工工程机械有限公司)
吕　伟(广西玉柴重工有限公司)　　　禄君胜(山推工程机械股份有限公司)

**秘　书　长** 丁润铎(人民交通出版社)

# 总 序

中国高等职业教育在教育部的积极推动下,经过10年的"示范"建设,现已进入"标准化"建设阶段。

2012年,教育部正式颁布了《高等职业学校专业教学标准》,解决了我国高等职业教育教什么、怎么教、教到什么程度的问题,为培养目标和规格、组织实施教学、规范教学管理、加强专业建设、开发教材和学习资源提供了依据。

目前,国内开设工程机械类专业的高等职业学校,大部分是原交通运输行业的院校,现为交通职业学院,而且这些院校大都是教育部"示范"建设学校。人民交通出版社审时度势,利用行业优势,集合院校10年示范建设的成果,组织国内近20所开设工程机械类专业高等职业教育院校专业负责人和骨干教师,于2012年4月在北京举行"示范院校工程机械专业教学教材改革研讨会"。本次会议的主要议题是交流示范院校工程机械专业人才培养工学结合成果、研讨工程机械专业课改教材开发。会议宣布成立教材编审委员会,张铁教授为首届主任委员。会议确定了8种专业平台课程、5种专业核心课程及6种专业拓展课程的主编、副主编。

2012年7月,高等职业教育工程机械类专业教材大纲审定会在山东交通学院顺利召开。各位主编分别就教材编写思路、编写模式、大纲内容、样章内容和课时安排进行了说明。会议确定了14门课程大纲,并就20门课程的编写进度与出版时间进行商定。此外,会议代表商议,教材定稿审稿会将按照专业平台课程、专业核心课程、专业拓展课程择时召开。

本教材的编写,以教育部《高等职业学校专业教学标准》为依据,以培养职业能力为主线,任务驱动、项目引领、问题启智,教、学、做一体化,既突出岗位实际,又不失工程机械技术前沿,同时将国内外一流工程机械的代表产品及工法、绿色节能技术等融入其中,使本套教材更加贴近市场,更加适应"用得上,下得去,干得好"的高素质技能人才的培养。

本套教材适用于教育部《高等职业学校专业教育标准》中规定的"工程机械控制技术(520109)"、"工程机械运用与维护(520110)"、"公路机械化施工技术(520112)"、"高等级公路维护与管理(520102)"、"道路桥梁工程技术(520108)"等专业。

本套教材也可作为工程机械制造企业、工程施工企业、公路桥梁施工及养护企业等职工培训教材。

本套教材也是广大工程机械技术人员难得的技术读本。

本套教材是工程机械类专业广大高等职业示范院校教师、专家智慧和辛勤劳动的结晶。在此向所有参编者表示敬意和感谢。

**高等职业教育工程机械类专业规划教材编审委员会**
2013 年 1 月

# 前 言

我国经济的高速发展、基础设施的建设规模逐步扩大的同时,也带动了我国工程机械行业的迅猛发展。许多国外知名的工程机械产品制造商纷纷加入我国市场,每年都有大量的信息和技术引入我国,这些都离不开英语,英语是信息沟通和交流的媒介和基础。为了适应形势的发展,作者编写了本书。

本教材为示范院校工程机械专业教学教材,全书分为10个项目,主要内容有:柴油发动机、柴油机燃油供给系统、发动机冷却系统和润滑系统、传动系统、发动机起动系统、液压系统、筑路机械、路面养护机械、设备维护、动态仿真技术在工程机械设计上的应用等内容。教材内容力求深入浅出,体现新知识、新技术和新方法,并适当留有供自学和拓宽专业的知识内容。教学内容图文并茂,直观生动,能增强教学的直观性与生动性,提高学生学习积极性。

本书由吴明华、陈晓娟任主编,杨川、李活任副主编,其中项目一~项目五由安徽交通职业技术学院吴明华编写,项目六由成都铁路学校杨川编写、项目七由江苏省交通技师学院李鹏飞编写,项目八~项目十由湖南交通职业技术学院陈晓娟、李活编写。全书由吴明华统稿,由安徽农业大学郁玉叶、北京建筑大学连香姣共同审定。

本书涉及知识面较广,编写过程中也力求准确无误,但由于水平所限,不妥之处在所难免,敬请读者批评指正。

编者

2014 年 4 月

# 目 录

**项目1 柴油发动机的认识** ································································· 1
    Project 1  Acquaintance with Diesel Engine ······································· 2
    Practical Reading ································································· 7

**项目2 柴油机燃油供给系统的认识** ················································· 11
    Project 2  Acquaintance with Diesel Engine Fuel System ······················ 12
    Practical Reading ································································ 18

**项目3 发动机冷却系统和润滑系统的认识** ······································ 21
    Project 3  Acquaintance with Engine Cooling and Lubricating System ······· 22
    Practical Reading ································································ 29

**项目4 传动系统的认识** ································································· 32
    Project 4  Acquaintance with Transmission System ······························· 33
    Practical Reading ································································ 46

**项目5 发动机起动系统的介绍** ······················································· 50
    Project 5  Introduction to the Starting System ···································· 50
    Practical Reading ································································ 53

**项目6 液压系统的介绍** ································································· 56
    Project 6  Introduction to Hydraulic Systems ····································· 57
    Practical Reading ································································ 61

**项目7 筑路机械的介绍** ································································· 66
    Project 7  Introduction to the Construction Machinery ·························· 66
    Practical Reading ································································ 75

**项目8 路面养护机械的介绍** ·························································· 79
    Project 8  Introduction to Pavement Maintenance Machinery ··················· 80
    Practical Reading ································································ 86

**项目9 设备维护的介绍** ································································· 90
    Project 9  Introduction to the Maintenance of Construction Machinery ······· 91
    Practical Reading ································································ 93

**项目10 动态仿真技术在工程机械设计上的应用** ······························ 96
    Project 10  Using Dynamic Simulation in the Development of Construction Machinery ······ 97
    Practical Reading ······························································· 100

**参考文献** ························································································ 102

# 项目 1
# 柴油发动机的认识

### 学习目标

完成本项目学习任务后,你应当能:
1. 认识关于柴油机的专业术语,熟悉柴油机的工作过程及发展状况;
2. 基于所学专业知识,借助专业词典能无障碍地查阅与柴油机相关的英语资料;
3. 正确完成课后练习。

### 任务描述

通过柴油机与汽油机的简单对比,完成相关单词、词汇、特殊语句的学习。对柴油机的工作特点、自身不足及其新技术有一定的认识。强化相关专业英文资料的阅读能力。

### 引导问题

说说柴油机与汽油机的区别。

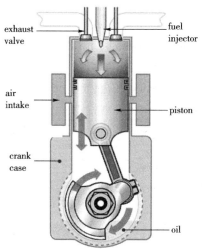

### 学 时

2 学时

# Project 1　Acquaintance with Diesel Engine

Diesel engines are mechanical devices that use controlled explosions (combustions) of diesel and air to rotate wheels. The reciprocating (back and forth) engine explodes the mixture (of diesel fuel + air) in a cylinder that forces the contained piston to move. This movement of the piston is transmitted (via the connecting rod) to a rotating device (crankshaft shown as a simple red disc) which is ultimately connected to the wheels (via gears, usually). The diesel engine is similar to the 4-stroke petrol engine. In theory, diesel engines and gasoline engines are quite similar. They are both internal combustion engines designed to convert the chemical energy available in fuel into mechanical energy. This mechanical energy moves pistons up and down inside cylinders. The pistons are connected to a crankshaft, and the up-and-down motion of the pistons, known as linear motion, creates the rotary motion needed to turn the wheels of a car forward.

Both diesel engines and gasoline engines covert fuel into energy through a series of small explosions or combustions. The major difference between diesel and gasoline is the way these explosions happen. In a gasoline engine, fuel is mixed with air, compressed by pistons and ignited by sparks from spark plugs. In a diesel engine, however, the air is compressed first, and then the fuel is injected. Because air heats up when it's compressed, the fuel ignites. The diesel engine therefore does not require a sparking plug. The diesel fuel (which is heavier and contains longer chain hydrocarbons) is injected directly into the cylinder when the air has been greatly heated by the compression stroke.

The diesel cycle goes like this:

1. When the piston is at the top of its travel, the cylinder contains a charge of highly compressed air. Diesel fuel is sprayed into the cylinder by the injector and immediately ignites because of the heat and pressure inside the cylinder.

The pressure created by the combustion of the fuel drives the piston downward. This is the power stroke (shown as Figure 1-1).

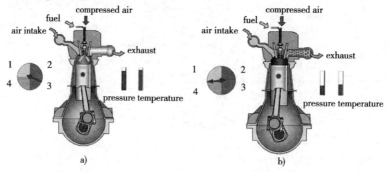

Figure 1-1　Power and Exhaust Stroke
a) fuel injection and combustion; b) exhaust

2. As the piston nears the bottom of its stroke, all of the exhaust valves open. Exhaust gases rush out of the cylinder, relieving the pressure (shown as Figure 1-1).

3. As the piston bottoms out, it uncovers the air intake ports. Pressurized air fills the cylinder, forcing out the remainder of the exhaust gases (shown as Figure 1-2).

4. The exhaust valves close and the piston starts traveling back upward, re-covering the intake ports and compressing the fresh charge of air. This is the compression stroke (shown as Figure 1-2).

5. As the piston nears the top of the cylinder, the cycle repeats with step 1.

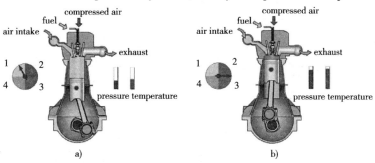

Figure 1-2 Intake and Compression Stroke
a) air intake; b) press

Diesel's story actually begins with the invention of the gasoline engine. Nikolaus August Otto had invented and patented the gasoline engine by 1876. This invention used the four-stroke combustion principle, also known as the "Otto Cycle", and it's the basic premise for most car engines today. In its early stage, the gasoline engine wasn't very efficient, and other major methods of transportation such as the steam engine fared poorly as well. Only about 10 percent of the fuel used in these types of engines actually moved a vehicle. The rest of the fuel simply produced useless heat.

In 1878, Rudolf Diesel was attending the Polytechnic High School of Germany (the equivalent of an engine ring college) when he learned about the low efficiency of gasoline and steam engines. This disturbing information inspired him to create an engine with a higher efficiency, and he devoted much of his time to developing a "Combustion Power Engine". By 1892 Diesel had obtained a patent for what we now call the diesel engine.

If diesel engines are so efficient, why don't we use them more often? You might see the words "diesel engine" and think of big, hefty cargo trucks spewing out black, sooty smoke and creating a loud clattering noise. This negative image of diesel trucks and engines has made diesel less attractive to casual drivers in theUnited States—although diesel is great for hauling large shipments over long distances, it hasn't been the best choice for everyday commuters.[①] This is starting to change, however, as people are improving the diesel engine to make it cleaner and less noisy.

**Today's Improved Diesel Engine Technology**

If you haven't driven a diesel powered car lately, you would be surprised at how much they have improved. Gone are clanking engines, smelly exhaust, and anemic performance.[②]

Diesel rattle is eliminated by a combination of direct injection (DI), common rail (CR) fuel distribution, unit fuel injectors, and pilot injection. With DI, fuel is injected directly into the cylinder rather than into a small side chamber as with older indirect injection (IDI). This helps provide the fine, high-pressure mist of fuel needed to eliminate knocks and rattles. High pressure also means better fuel atomization, resulting in increased engine efficiency for more power and better fuel economy (shown as Figure 1-3).

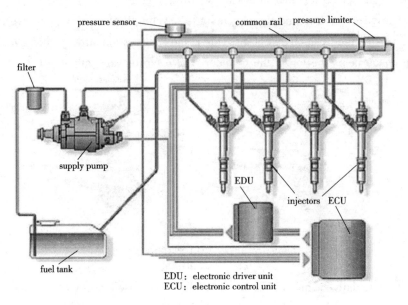

Figure 1-3    Direct Injection and Common Rail

The common rail system uses an engine-driven pump that produces extremely high pressure fuel delivered to the electrically-operated injector at each cylinder, via a single thick-walled tube——the "common rail." Besides reducing characteristic diesel noise, the CR system can greatly increase injection pressure over the older distributor pump type of injection systems, thus injecting a far finer mist of fuel to enhance DI engine efficiency.

Diesel fuel has to be injected at very high pressures to counter the huge compression pressure in the diesel engine. The higher the pressure, the more power is produced and the cleaner the exhaust emissions. Another advancement is pilot injection, which injects a small amount of fuel prior to the main injection, resulting in a more gradual increase in combustion chamber temperature. This eliminates the diesel knocking and rattling caused by a sudden increase in temperature. All this is made possible by sophisticated electronic injection control systems.

Today's diesel engines are usually turbocharged and most are intercooled. Turbochargers compress the air supplied to the engine, or in automotive terms, improve engine "breathing." More air means more fuel can be combusted, leading to increased power output. Exhaust gases spin the turbocharger's turbine at speeds of up to 150,000 rpm, which rotates an air pump that provides a "boost" of air higher than atmospheric pressure for more powerful combustion. Because the turbocharger is driven by engine exhaust, temperatures are very high. Countering this is an intercooler, either an air-to-air or water-to-air heat exchanger, that's used to cool down the hot compressed air exiting the turbocharger. Cooler air takes up less volume, so more air can be delivered to the cylinders to produce more power.

Recognizing American's demand for vehicles offering good fuel economy without compromising utility, cargo capacity, and performance, Mercedes-Benz is one of those leading the way by offering several diesel models. The E320 CDI, which has been offered for several years, has been replaced by the E320 BLUETEC luxury sedan. The E320 BLUETEC is the only diesel-powered luxury sedan available in the U.S. that can deliver an estimated 780 miles on a tank of fuel. In addition, there is the new ML320 CDI, R320 CDI, and GL320 CDI-all SUVs. As of now, these four diesel models are not available in California, Maine, Maryland, New York, and Vermont because they do not pass the more stringent emission requirements in these five states.

The Department of Energy estimates that a 30 percent market penetration of light-duty diesel vehicles by 2020 would reduce U.S. net crude oil imports by 350,000 barrels per day. In California alone, gradually increasing the use of currently-available clean diesel technology in cars, pickups, and SUVs to levels seen today in Europe could save the state 110 million gallons of gasoline per year by 2010, and up to 840 million gallons per year by 2030.

Diesel is on the rise in America: The forces holding it back-namely long-held stigmas and emissions concerns - are quickly being overcome by technology and now, of course, cleaner diesel fuel.

A new generation of clean diesel vehicles selling in large numbers opens the door for biodiesel to play a bigger role as well. This clean-burning fuel is derived from domestically produced agricultural products and runs in a diesel engine with little or no modifications, reducing both emissions and energy dependence.

Plus, diesels could factor favorably into the future of the popular hybrid as well. Just imagine the fuel economy that could be achieved by combining the fuel-saving benefits of hybrid-electric technology with an inherently efficient diesel engine. For example, Daimler Chrysler has developed a "mild hybrid" that combines the 3-liter BLUETEC V-6 diesel with a high-torque electric motor. With all this potential, we expect to be hearing a lot more about diesel in the years ahead.

## Word List

1. mechanical [mi'kænikəl]　　　　　n. 机械的, 机械学的
2. explosion [iks'pləuʒən]　　　　　n. 爆炸
3. combustion [kəm'bʌstʃən]　　　　n. 燃烧
4. reciprocating [ri'siprəkeitiŋ]　　　n. (机器的部件)直线往复运动
5. cylinder ['silində]　　　　　　　n. 汽缸
6. piston ['pistən]　　　　　　　　n. 活塞
7. crankshaft ['kræŋkʃɑ:ft]　　　　　n. (内燃机的)曲轴
8. stroke [strəuk]　　　　　　　　n. 行程, 冲程
9. available [ə'veiləbəl]　　　　　　a. 可利用的, 可得到的
10. convert [kən'və:t, 'kɔnvə:t]　　　v. (使)转变(化)
11. linear ['liniə]　　　　　　　　adj. 直线的, 线形的
12. rotary ['rəutəri]　　　　　　　adj. 旋转的
13. ignite [ig'nait]　　　　　　　　vt. 点燃, 使燃烧
14. plug [plʌg]　　　　　　　　　n. (内燃机的)火花塞
15. sparking ['spɑ:kiŋ]　　　　　　n. 发火花, 打火花

16. generate [ˈdʒenəreit]        vt. 产生
17. theory [ˈθiəri]               n. 理论，原理
18. inject [inˈdʒekt]             vt. (给…)注射
19. spray                         vt. & vi. 喷，喷射
                                  n. 喷雾
20. charge [tʃɑːdʒ]               n. (带电物质的)电荷，充电量
21. invention [inˈvenʃən]         n. 发明
22. patent [ˈpeitənt]             vt. 获得……专利
23. premise [ˈpremis]             n. 前提
24. fare [fɛə]                    vi. 进展，遭遇
25. polytechnic [ˌpɔliːˈteknik]   n. 工艺学校，综合性工艺学校，理工专科学校
26. wheel [hwiːl]                 n. 轮子
27. travel [ˈtrævəl]              n. 旅行，进行
28. equivalent [iˈkwivələnt]      adj. 相等的，相当的，等效的
29. engineering [ˌendʒiˈniəriŋ]   n. 工程
30. disturbing [diˈstəːbiŋ, diˈstɜrbiŋ]  adj. 烦扰的，令人不安的
31. inspire [inˈspaiə]            vt. 鼓舞，激励，赋予灵感
32. hefty [ˈhefti]                adj. 重的，健壮的，异常大的
                                  n. 健壮的人
33. cargo [ˈkɑːgəu]               n. (船或飞机装载的)货物，负荷，荷重
34. spew [spjuː]                  vt. & vi. 喷出
35. anemic [əˈniːmik]             adj. 没有活力的，无精打采的
36. atomization [ˌætəmaiˈzeiʃən]  n. 雾化
37. rattle [ˈrætl]                n. 嘎嘎声，发出嘎嘎声的儿童玩具

## Proper Names

1. 4-stroke petrol engine         四冲程汽油机
2. sparking plug                  火花塞
3. Otto Cycle                     奥托循环
4. power stroke                   做功行程
5. compression stroke             压缩行程
6. long chain hydrocarbon         长链碳氢化合物
7. unit fuel injector             整体式喷油器
8. pilot injector                 引燃喷射

## Notes

①This negative image of diesel trucks and engines has made diesel less attractive to casual drivers in the United States—although diesel is great for hauling large shipments over long distances, it hasn't been the best choice for everyday commuters.

柴油机和柴油车的这个负面印象使得美国的驾驶者对其不怎么感兴趣。虽然柴油车在长

途大宗货物运输中很有用,但它还不是日常通勤者的最佳选择。

②Gone are clanking engines, smelly exhaust, and anemic performance.

当啷当啷的发动机、难闻的废气、动力不够强劲,在柴油机上已不复存在。

### Exercises

**1. Choose the best answer from the following choices according to the text.**

_____: piston moves down, air + diesel fuel mixture drawn in. _____: piston moves up, air + fuel mixture compressed until it explodes. _____: piston pushed down by exploding air + fuel mixture. _____: piston moves up, spent gases pushed out through exhaust.

A. INTAKE    B. COMPRESSION    C. EXHAUST    D. POWER

**2. Translate the following into Chinese.**

1) diesel engine    2) direct injection    3) fuel injectors

**3. Translate the following into English.**

1) 燃烧    2) 行程    3) 转换

# Practical Reading

## Internal Combustion Engine

### 内燃机认识

A car engine is an internal combustion engine—combustion takes place internally. There are different kinds of internal combustion engines. Diesel engines are one form and gas turbine engines are another. See also the articles on HEMI engines, rotary engines and two-stroke engines. ①Each has its own advantages and disadvantages.

There is such a thing as an external combustion engine. A steam engine in old-fashioned trains and steam boats is the best example of an external combustion engine. The fuel (coal, wood, oil, whatever) in a steam engine burns outside the engine to create steam, and the steam creates motion inside the engine. Internal combustion is a lot more efficient (takes less fuel per mile) than external combustion, plus an internal combustion engine is a lot smaller than an equivalent external combustion engine. This explains why we don't see any cars from Ford and GM using steam engines.

The principle behind any reciprocating internal combustion engine: If you put a tiny amount of high-energy fuel (like gasoline) in a small, enclosed space and ignite it, an incredible amount of energy is released in the form of expanding gas. Almost all cars currently use what is called a four-stroke combustion cycle to convert gasoline into motion. The four-stroke approach is also known as the Otto cycle, in honor of Nikolaus Otto, who invented it in 1867. The four strokes are intake stroke, compression stroke, combustion stroke and exhaust stroke.

Notice that the motion that comes out of an internal combustion engine is rotational. In an engine the linear motion of the pistons is converted into rotational motion by the crankshaft. The rotational motion is nice because we plan to turn (rotate) the car's wheels with it anyway.

## Basic Engine Parts (shown as Figure 1-4)

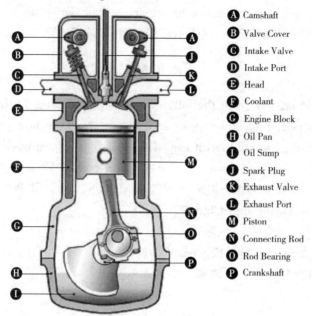

- **A** Camshaft
- **B** Valve Cover
- **C** Intake Valve
- **D** Intake Port
- **E** Head
- **F** Coolant
- **G** Engine Block
- **H** Oil Pan
- **I** Oil Sump
- **J** Spark Plug
- **K** Exhaust Valve
- **L** Exhaust Port
- **M** Piston
- **N** Connecting Rod
- **O** Rod Bearing
- **P** Crankshaft

Figure 1-4 The Structure of the Internal Combustion Engine

The core of the engine is the cylinder, with the piston moving up and down inside the cylinder. The engine described above has one cylinder. That is typical of most lawn mowers, but most cars have more than one cylinder (four, six and eight cylinders are common). In a multi-cylinder engine, the cylinders usually are arranged in one of three ways: inline, V or flat (also known as horizontally opposed or boxer)[2] (shown as Figure 1-5).

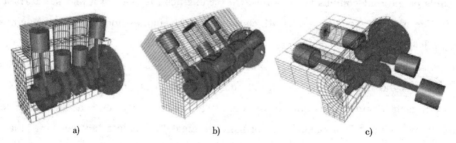

Figure 1-5 The Arrangement of Cylinders
a) inline; b) type; c) flat

Different configurations have different advantages and disadvantages in terms of smoothness, manufacturing cost and shape characteristics. These advantages and disadvantages make them more suitable for certain vehicles.

Let's look at some key engine parts in more detail.

### Spark Plug

The spark plug supplies the spark that ignites the air/fuel mixture so that combustion can occur. The spark must happen at just the right moment for things to work properly.

### Valves

The intake and exhaust valves open at the proper time to let in air and fuel and to let out exhaust. Note that both valves are closed during compression and combustion so that the combustion chamber is sealed.

**Piston**

A piston is a cylindrical piece of metal that moves up and down inside the cylinder.

**Piston Rings**

Piston rings provide a sliding seal between the outer edge of the piston and the inner edge of the cylinder. The rings serve two purposes:

They prevent the fuel/air mixture and exhaust in the combustion chamber from leaking into the sump during compression and combustion.

They keep oil in the sump from leaking into the combustion area, where it would be burned and lost.

**Connecting Rod**

The connecting rod connects the piston to the crankshaft. It can rotate at both ends so that its angle can change as the piston moves and the crankshaft rotates.

**Crankshaft**

The crankshaft turns the piston's up and down motion into circular motion just like a crank on a jack-in-the-box does.

**Sump**

The sump surrounds the crankshaft. It contains some amount of oil, which collects in the bottom of the sump (the oil pan).

## Word List

1. advantage [əd'vɑ:ntidʒ]    *n.* 有利条件,益处,优越(性)
2. external [eks'tə:nl]    *adj.* 外面的,外部的
3. plus [plʌs]    *prep.* (表示运算)加;(表示包容)外加
4. incredible [in'kredəbl]    *adj.* 不可思议的;惊人的;难以置信的
5. crankshaft ['kræŋkʃɑ:ft]    *n.* (内燃机的)曲轴,曲柄轴

## Proper Names

1. HEMI engine    半球形燃烧室的发动机
2. in honor of    为了向…表示敬意
3. lawn mowers    草坪割草机

## Notes

①See also the articles on HEMI engines, rotary engines and two-stroke engines.

hemispherical combustion chamber engine 可缩写为 HEMI engine。可关闭一半汽缸保留另一半汽缸工作是当今 HEMI 发动机的一个显著特征,然而,HEMI 发动机最基本的特征应该是拥有半球形燃烧室汽缸结构。

②In a multi-cylinder engine, the cylinders usually are arranged in one of three ways: inline, V or flat (also known as horizontally opposed or boxer).

对多缸发动机而言,汽缸的分布形式有三种:直列式、V形和卧式(也可称为水平对置式或水平对卧式)。

## 参考答案

**1. Choose the best answer from the following choices according to the text.**

A　B　D　C

**2. Translate the following into Chinese.**

1)柴油机　　　2)直喷　　　3)燃油喷油器

**3. Translate the following into English.**

1)combustion　　2)stroke　　3)convert

# 项目 2

# 柴油机燃油供给系统的认识

## 学习目标

完成本项目学习任务后,你应当能:

1. 认识关于柴油机燃油供给系统的专业术语,熟悉其组成及工作过程;
2. 基于所学专业知识,借助专业词典能无障碍地查阅与柴油机燃油供给系统相关的英语资料;
3. 正确完成课后练习。

## 任务描述

完成相关单词、词汇、特殊语句的学习,强化柴油机燃油供给系统相关专业英文资料的阅读能力。

## 引导问题

参考下图,说说柴油机燃油供给系统的组成。

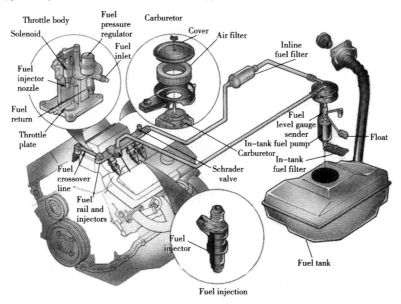

## Project 2　Acquaintance with Diesel Engine Fuel System

The function of the fuel system is to store and supply fuel to the cylinder chamber where it can be mixed with air, vaporized, and burned to produce energy. The diesel is stored in a fuel tank. A fuel pump draws the fuel from the tank through fuel lines and delivers it through a fuel filter to either a carburetor or fuel injector, then delivered to the cylinder chamber for combustion[①]( shown as Figure 2-1).

So, fuel control can be divided into two elements: First, through a variety of electrically driven components, the hydraulic function of the system ensures that clean pressurized fuel is available at the injectors. The second element, fuel control, is accomplished by monitoring INPUT signals from sensors reflecting vehicle and engine operating conditions and driver demands. From this information the computer uses its program to compute how long to hold each injector open. This OUPUT is referred to as pulse width. The resulting combustion byproducts are monitored by the oxygen sensor. Using this INPUT as a correction, pulse width is recomputed for the next cylinder.

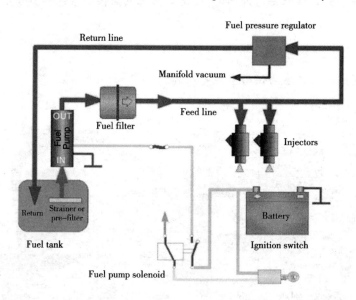

Figure 2-1　Fuel Control of the Diesel Engine Fuel System

### Fuel Pump

A fuel pump is a frequently (but not always) essential component on internal combustion engined device. Many engines (older motorcycle engines in particular) do not require any fuel pump at all, requiring only gravity to feed fuel from the fuel tank through a line or hose to the engine. ②But in non-gravity feed designs, fuel has to be pumped from the fuel tank to the engine and delivered under low pressure to the carburetor or under high pressure to the fuel injection system. Often, carbureted engines use low pressure mechanical pumps that are mounted outside the fuel tank, whereas fuel injected engines often use electric fuel pumps that are mounted inside the fuel tank (and some fuel injected engines have two fuel pumps: one low pressure/high volume supply pump in the tank and one high pressure/low volume pump on or near the engine).

**Carburetors**

A carburetor basically consists of an open pipe through which the air passes into the inlet manifold of the engine. The pipe is in the form of a venturi: it narrows in section and then widens again, causing the airflow to increase in speed in the narrowest part. ③Below the venturi is a butterfly valve called the throttle valve — a rotating disc that can be turned end-on to the airflow, so as to hardly restrict the flow at all, or can be rotated so that it (almost) completely blocks the flow of air. This valve controls the flow of air through the carburetor throat and thus the quantity of air/fuel mixture the system will deliver, thereby regulating engine power and speed. The throttle is connected, usually through a cable or a mechanical linkage of rods and joints, to the accelerator pedal on a car or the equivalent control on other vehicles or equipment (shown as Figure 2-2).

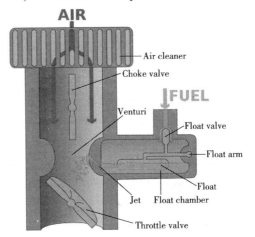

Figure 2-2 Basic Carburetor

Fuel is introduced into the air stream through small holes at the narrowest part of the venturi and at other places where pressure will be lowered when not running on full throttle. Fuel flow is adjusted by means of precisely calibrated orifices, referred to as jets, in the fuel path.

So, the carburetor works on Bernoulli's principle: the faster air moves, the lower its static pressure, and the higher its dynamic pressure. ④The throttle (accelerator) linkage does not directly control the flow of liquid fuel. Instead, it actuates carburetor mechanisms which meter the flow of air being pulled into the engine. The speed of this flow, and therefore its pressure, determines the amount of fuel drawn into the airstream.

The main disadvantage of basing a carburetor's operation on Bernoulli's principle is that, being a fluid dynamic device, the pressure reduction in a venturi tends to be proportional to the square of the intake air speed. The fuel jets are much smaller and limited mainly by viscosity, so that the fuel flow tends to be proportional to the pressure difference. So jets sized for full power tend to starve the engine at lower speed and part throttle. Most commonly this has been corrected by using multiple jets. In other movable jet carburetors, it was corrected by varying the jet size. For cold starting, a different principle was used in multi-jet carburetors. A flow resisting valve called a choke, similar to the throttle valve, was placed upstream of the main jet to reduce the intake pressure and suck additional fuel out of the jets.

**Common Rail**(shown as Figure 2-3)

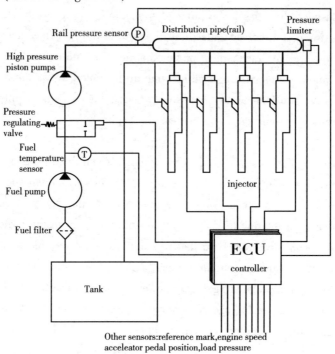

Figure 2-3  Common Rail

Solenoid or piezoelectric valves make possible fine electronic control over the fuel injection time and quantity, and the higher pressure that the common rail technology makes available provides better fuel atomization. ⑤In order to lower engine noise, the engine's electronic control unit can inject a small amount of diesel just before the main injection event ("pilot" injection), thus reducing its explosiveness and vibration, as well as optimizing injection timing and quantity for variations in fuel quality, cold starting and so on. Some advanced common rail fuel systems perform as many as five injections per stroke.

Common rail engines require very short ( <10 second) or no heating-up time at all, dependent on ambient temperature, and produce lower engine noise and emissions than older systems.

In common rail systems, a high-pressure pump stores a reservoir of fuel at high pressure-up to and above 2,000 bars (29,000 psi). The term "common rail" refers to the fact that all of the fuel injectors are supplied by a common fuel rail which is nothing more than a pressure accumulator where the fuel is stored at high pressure. This accumulator supplies multiple fuel injectors with high-pressure fuel. This simplifies the purpose of the high-pressure pump in that it only has to maintain a commanded pressure at a target (either mechanically or electronically controlled). The fuel injectors are typically ECU-controlled. When the fuel injectors are electrically activated, a hydraulic valve (consisting of a nozzle and plunger) is mechanically or hydraulically opened and fuel is sprayed into the cylinders at the desired pressure. Since the fuel pressure energy is stored remotely and the injectors are electrically actuated, the injection pressure at the start and end of injection is very near the pressure in the accumulator (rail), thus producing a square injection rate. If the accumulator, pump and plumbing are sized properly, the injection pressure and rate will be the same for each of the multiple injection events.

### Injector

Design of the Unit Injector eliminates the need for high pressure fuel pipes, and with that their associated failures, as well as allowing for much higher injection pressure to occur. The unit injector system allows accurate injection timing, and amount control as in the common rail system.

The Unit Injector is fitted into the engine cylinder head, where the fuel is supplied via integral ducts machined directly into the cylinder head. Each injector has its own pumping element, and in the case of electronic control, a fuel solenoid valve as well. The fuel system is divided into the low pressure (<500kPa) fuel supply system, and the high pressure injection system (<2000kPa).

The basic operation can be described as a sequence of four separate phases: the filling phase, the spill phase, the injection phase, and the pressure reduction phase.

A low pressure fuel delivery pump supplies filtered diesel fuel into the cylinder head fuel ducts, and into each injector fuel port of constant stroke pump plunger injector, which is overhead camshaft operated.

### Fill Phase

The constant stroke pump element on the way up draws fuel from the supply duct in to the chamber, and as long as electric solenoid valve remains de-energized fuel line is open.

### Spill Phase

The pump element is on the way down, and as long as solenoid valve remains de-energized the fuel line is open and fuel flows in through into the return duct.

### Injection Phase (shown as Figure 2-4)

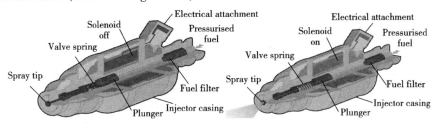

Figure 2-4  The Basic Injector

The pump element is still on the way down, the solenoid is now energized and fuel line is now closed. The fuel can not pass back into return duct, and is now compressed by the plunger until pressure exceeds specific "opening" pressure, and the injector nozzle needle lifts, allowing fuel to be injected into the combustion chamber.

### Pressure Reduction Phase

The plunger is still on its way down, the engine ECU de-energizes the solenoid when required quantity of fuel is delivered, the fuel valve opens, fuel can flow back into return duct, causing pressure drop, which in turn causes the injector nozzle needle to shut, hence no more fuel is injected.

### Summary

The start of an injection is controlled by the solenoid closing point, and the injected fuel quantity is determined by the closing time, which is the length of time the solenoid remains closed. The solenoid operation is fully controlled by the engine ECU.

**Fuel System Maintenance Tips**

- Change fuel filter every 20,000miles or 1 year
- Clean idle passage every 20,000miles
- Clean throttle blades every 20,000miles
- Clean back of fuel distributor plate (primarily on German manufactured vehicles) every 20,000miles
- Check air temperature sensor at 10,000miles
- Check throttle bolt torque (if applicable) at 20,000miles
- Check fuel lines for signs of deterioration and cracking every 2 years or 20,000miles
- Change oxygen sensor every 30,000miles
- Clean fuel injectors every 30,000miles

## Word List

1. byproduct ['baɪˌprɔdʌkt]    n. 副产品
2. monitor ['mɔnitə]    n. 显示屏,屏幕
      vt. 监控,监听
      vi. 监视
3. oxygen ['ɔksidʒən]    n. [化]氧,氧气
4. sensor ['sensə, -ˌsɔː]    n. 传感器
5. gravity ['græviti]    n. 重力
6. hose [həuz]    n. 软管
7. carburetor ['kɑːbjuretə]    n. 〈机〉汽化器,化油器
8. venturi [ven'tuəri]    n. 文氏管,文丘里管,一种流体流量测定装置
9. end-on ['end'ɔn]    adj. 在端点的
10. restrict [ris'trikt]    vt. 限制,限定;约束
11. block [blɔk]    vt. 阻止,阻塞;限制
12. equivalent [i'kwivələnt]    adj. 相等的,相当的,等效的
13. starve [stɑːv]    vi. 挨饿
       vt. 使挨饿
14. calibrate ['kæləˌbreɪt]    vt. 校准;使标准化
15. manifold ['mænəˌfəuld]    n. 歧管(汽车引擎用于进气或排气)
16. proportional [prə'pɔːʃənəl]    adj. 比例的,成比例的
17. choke [tʃəuk]    n. (车辆发动机的)阻风门
18. thereby ['ðɛəbai]    adv. 由此,从而
19. cable ['keibl]    n. 缆绳
20. rarely ['rɛəli]    adv. 很少地;罕有地
21. component [kəm'pəunənt]    n. 成分;零件
22. hydraulic [haɪ'drɔːlɪk]    adj. 水力的,水压的;用水发动的
23. piezoelectric [paiˌiːzəui'lektrik]    adj. 压电的
24. whereas [hwɛər'æz]    conj. 鉴于;然而

25. volume ['vɔlju:m]　　　　　　　　*n.* 量,大量
26. section ['sekʃən]　　　　　　　　*n.* 部分;节;部件;部门
27. orifice ['ɔ:rəfɪs, 'ɔr-]　　　　　*n.* 孔;洞口常见度:
28. jet [dʒet]　　　　　　　　　　　*n.* 喷嘴,喷雾
　　　　　　　　　　　　　　　　　　*vt.* 喷射,喷出
29. via ['vaɪə]　　　　　　　　　　　*prep.* 经过;通过,凭借
30. de-energize [ˌdi:'enədʒaɪz]　　　 *vt.* 断开(电源)
31. bolt [bəʊlt]　　　　　　　　　　 *n.* 螺栓,螺钉
32. deteriorate [dɪ'tɪərɪəreɪt]　　　 *vt.* 使恶化
　　　　　　　　　　　　　　　　　　*vi.* 恶化,变坏
33. crack [kræk]　　　　　　　　　　 *vt.* 破裂,打开;(使……)开裂

## Proper Names

1. solenoid valve　　　　　　　电磁阀,螺线管操纵阀
2. Bernoulli's principle　　　　伯努利原理
3. by means of　　　　　　　　 用,依靠
4. throttle valve　　　　　　　 节流阀
5. butterfly valve　　　　　　　蝶形阀
6. gravity feed　　　　　　　　 重力自流进料
7. pulse width　　　　　　　　 脉冲宽度,脉冲持续时间
8. a variety of　　　　　　　　 多种的
9. constant stroke pump　　　　 定行程泵

## Notes

①A fuel pump draws the fuel from the tank through fuel lines and delivers it through a fuel filter to either a carburetor or fuel injector, then delivered to the cylinder chamber for combustion.
燃油泵从油箱吸油,油经燃油管道及燃油过滤器输送到化油器或者燃油喷油器,然后再被输送到汽缸燃烧室燃烧。

②Many engines (older motorcycle engines in particular) do not require any fuel pump at all, requiring only gravity to feed fuel from the fuel tank through a line or hose to the engine.
许多发动机(尤其是老式的摩托车发动机)根本不需要燃油泵,仅靠重力自流作用通过燃油管道或软管从油箱给发动机供油。

③The pipe is in the form of a venturi: it narrows in section and then widens again, causing the airflow to increase in speed in the narrowest part.
管子是文丘里管的形式:部分变窄然后又放宽,使得气流在最窄的部位加快速度。

④So, the carburetor works on Bernoulli's principle: the faster air moves, the lower its static pressure, and the higher its dynamic pressure.
化油器的工作基于伯努利原理:空气流速越快,静压力越低,它的动压力越高。

⑤Solenoid or piezoelectric valves make possible fine electronic control over the fuel injection time and quantity, and the higher pressure that the common rail technology makes available provides better fuel atomization.

螺线管或压电阀尽可能对喷油时间和喷油量进行良好的电子控制,共轨技术所有的更高油压提供更好的燃油雾化效果。

## Exercises

**1. Choose the best answer from the following choices according to the text.**

1) The unit _____ system allows accurate injection timing, and amount control as in the common rail system.

 A. carburetor    B. injector    C. crankshaft    D. camshaft

2) It narrows in section and then widens again, causing the airflow to increase in speed in the _____ part.

 A. widest    B. biggest    C. narrowest    D. smallest

3) The _____ of this flow, and therefore its pressure, determines the amount of fuel drawn into the airstream.

 A. power    B. speed    C. friction    D. amount

4) The _____ is still on its way down, the engine ECU de-energizes the solenoid when required quantity of fuel is delivered, the fuel valve opens, fuel can flow back into return duct, causing pressure drop, which in turn causes the injector nozzle needle to shut, hence no more fuel is injected.

 A. plunger    B. valve    C. cylinder    D. linkage

**2. Translate the following into Chinese**

 1) carburetor    2) throttle body    3) fuel injector nozzle

# Practical Reading

## Diesel Fuel

## 柴油

The word "diesel" is derived from the family name of German inventor Rudolf Diesel who in 1892 invented the diesel engine. Diesel fuel, like gasoline is a complex blend of carbon and hydrogen compounds. It too requires additives for maximum performance. There are two grades of diesel fuel used in automobiles today: 1-D and 2-D. Number 2 diesel fuel has a lower volatility and is blended for higher loads and steady speeds, therefore works best in large truck applications. Because number 2 diesel fuel is less volatile, it tends to create hard starting in cold weather. On the other hand, number 1 diesel is more volatile, and therefore more suitable for use in an automobile, where there are constant changes in load and speed. Since diesel fuel vaporizes at a much higher temperature than gasoline, there is no need for a fuel evaporation control system as with gasoline. Diesel fuels are rated with a cetane number rather than an octane number. While a higher octane of gasoline indicates resistance to ignition, the higher cetane rating of diesel fuel indicates the ease at which the fuel will ignite. ①Most number 1 diesel fuels have a cetane rating of 50, while number 2 diesel fuels have a rating of 45. Diesel fuel emissions are higher in sulfur, and lower in carbon monoxide and hydrocarbons than gasoline and are subject to different emission testing standards.

**Reduction of Sulfur Emissions**

In the past, diesel fuel contained higher quantities of sulfur. European emission standards and preferential taxation have forced oil refineries to dramatically reduce the level of sulfur in diesel fuels. In the United States, more stringent emission standards have been adopted with the transition to ULSD starting in 2006, and becoming mandatory on June 1, 2010 (see also diesel exhaust). U.S. diesel fuel typically also has a lower cetane number (a measure of ignition quality) than European diesel, resulting in worse cold weather performance and some increase in emissions.

**Use as Car Fuel**

Diesel-powered cars generally have a better fuel economy than equivalent gasoline engines and produce less greenhouse gas emission. Their greater economy is due to the higher energy per-litre content of diesel fuel and the intrinsic efficiency of the diesel engine. While petrodiesel's higher density results in higher greenhouse gas emissions per litre compared to gasoline, the 20-40percent better fuel economy achieved by modern diesel-engined automobiles offsets the higher per-litre emissions of greenhouse gases, and a diesel-powered vehicle emits 10-20 percent less greenhouse gas than comparable gasoline vehicles. Biodiesel-powered diesel engines offer substantially improved emission reductions compared to petrodiesel or gasoline-powered engines, while retaining most of the fuel economy advantages over conventional gasoline-powered automobiles. However, the increased compression ratios mean there are increased emissions of oxides of nitrogen ($NO_x$) from diesel engines. This is compounded by biological nitrogen in biodiesel to make $NO_x$ emissions the main drawback of diesel versus gasoline engines.

# Word List

1. derive [diˈraiv]   vt. & vi. 得到,导出;源于,来自
2. blend [blend]   n. 混合;混合色,合成语;混合物
   vt. 混合;把…掺在一起;(使)调和
3. additive [ˈæditiv]   n. 添加剂
4. volatility [ˌvɔləˈtiliti]   n. 挥发性
5. volatile [ˈvɔlətail]   adj. 不稳定的;(液体或油)易挥发的
6. constant [ˈkɔnstənt]   adj. 不断的;永恒的;坚定;忠实的
   n. 〈数〉常数,常量;不变的事物;永恒值
7. vaporize [ˈveipəraiz]   vt. & vi. (使)蒸发,(使)气化
8. evaporation [iˌvæpəˈreiʃən]   n. 蒸发,发散;消失
9. rate [reit]   vt. 估价;值得;责骂;定级
   vt. & vi. 认为,把…算作
10. cetane [ˈsiːtein]   n. 十六烷
11. octane [ˈɔktein]   n. 辛烷
12. indicate [ˈindikeit]   vt. 表明

13. sulfur ['sʌlfə]      n. 硫磺
14. carbon monoxide ['ka:bən məunɔk'said]      n. 一氧化物
15. hydrocarbons ['haidrəuka:bənz]      n. 〈化〉碳氢化合物,烃
16. reduction [ri'dʌkʃn]      n. 减少;降低
17. preferential [,prefə'renʃəl]      adj. 优先的;优先选择的
18. taxation [tæk'seiʃn]      n. 课税;征税;税;税收
19. refinery [ri'fainəri:]      n. 精炼厂;精炼设备;提炼厂
20. stringent ['strindʒənt]      adj. 严格的;迫切的
21. transition [træn'ziʃən]      n. 过渡,转变
22. mandatory ['mændə:tɔ:ri:]      adj. 强制的;命令的
23. equivalent [i'kwivələnt]      adj. 相等的,相当的
24. litre ['li:tə]      n. (容量单位)升
25. intrinsic [in'trinsik]      adj. 固有的,内在的,本质的
26. offset ['ɔfset]      vt. 抵消;补偿
27. density ['densiti]      n. 密度;稠密,浓厚;〈物〉浓度,比重
28. substantial [səb'stænʃəl]      adj. 充实的;实质的,真正的;有实力的
29. versus ['və:səs]      prep. (表示两队或双方对阵)对

## Proper Names

1. biodiesel      生物柴油
2. Rudolf Diesel      鲁道夫狄塞尔
3. greenhouse gas      二氧化碳、甲烷等导致温室效应的气体
4. be adopted with      被接受;被采用
5. be subject to      受支配;从属于
6. ULSD      ultra-low-sulfur diesel (ultra 过激的,极端的) 超低硫柴油

## Notes

①While a higher octane of gasoline indicates resistance to ignition, the higher cetane rating of diesel fuel indicates the ease at which the fuel will ignite.
汽油的辛烷值越高意味着燃烧越缓慢,然而,柴油的十六烷值越高则越容易燃烧。

## 参考答案

**1. Choose the best answer from the following choices according to the text.**
B   C   B   A

**2. Translate the following into Chinese.**
1)化油器      2)节气门体      3)喷油嘴

# 项目 3
# 发动机冷却系统和润滑系统的认识

**学习目标**

完成本项目学习任务后,你应当能:
1. 认识关于冷却系统和润滑系统的专业术语,熟悉其工作过程及发展状况;
2. 基于所学专业知识,借助专业词典的帮助能无障碍地查阅与冷却系统和润滑系统相关的英语资料;
3. 正确完成课后练习。

**任务描述**

通过学习冷却系统和润滑系统的组成,完成相关单词、词汇、特殊语句的学习。强化相关专业英文资料的阅读能力。

**引导问题**

分析图片中箭头的流向。

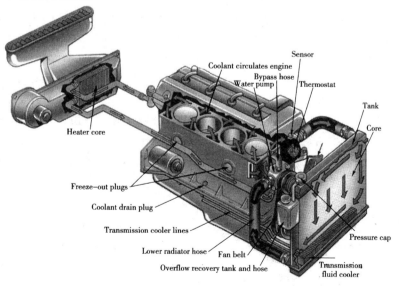

**学 时**

2 学时

# Project 3  Acquaintance with Engine Cooling and Lubricating System

## Cooling System

Today's cooling system must maintain the engine at a constant temperature whether the outside air temperature is 110 degrees Fahrenheit or 10 below zero. If the engine temperature is too low, fuel economy will suffer and emissions will rise. If the temperature is allowed to get too hot for too long, the engine will self destruct.

**How Does a Cooling System Work?**

Actually, there are two types of cooling systems found on machines: liquid cooled and air cooled. Many modern machines still use air cooling, but for the most part, automobiles and trucks use liquid cooled systems.

The cooling system is made up of the passages inside the engine block and heads, a water pump to circulate the coolant, a thermostat to control the temperature of the coolant, a radiator to cool the coolant, a radiator cap to control the pressure in the system, and some plumbing consisting of interconnecting hoses to transfer the coolant from the engine to radiator and also to the machine's heater system where hot coolant is used to warm up the machine's interior on a cold day.①

The coolant follows a path that takes it from the water pump, through passages inside the engine block where it collects the heat produced by the cylinders. It then flows up to the cylinder head where it collects more heat from the combustion chambers. It then flows out past the thermostat (if the thermostat is opened to allow the fluid to pass), through the upper radiator hose and into the radiator. The coolant flows through the thin flattened tubes that make up the core of the radiator and is cooled by the air flow through the radiator. From there, it flows out of the radiator, through the lower radiator hose and back to the water pump. By this time, the coolant is cooled off and ready to collect more heat from the engine. The water pump has the job of keeping the fluid moving through this system of plumbing and hidden passages (shown as Figure 3-1).

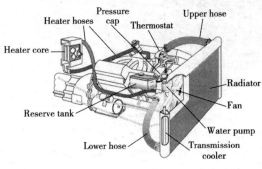

Figure 3-1  The Cooling System

The capacity of the system is engineered for the type and size of the engine and the work load that it is expected to undergo. Obviously, the cooling system for a larger, more powerful V8 engine in a heavy machine will need considerably more capacity than a compact machine with a small 4-cylinder engine. On a large machine, the radiator is larger with many more tubes for the coolant to flow through. The radiator is also wider and taller to capture more air flow entering the vehicle from the grill in front.

**The Radiator**

The radiator core is usually made of flattened aluminum tubes with aluminum strips that zigzag between the tubes. These fins transfer the heat in the tubes into the air stream to be carried away from the machine. On each end of the radiator core is a tank, usually made of plastic that covers the ends of the radiator (shown as Figure 3-2).

Figure 3-2  The Radiator Cooling Fan

On most modern radiators, the tubes run horizontally with the plastic tank on either side. On other machines, the tubes run vertically with the tank on the top and bottom. On older machines, the core was made of copper and the tanks were brass. The new aluminum-plastic system is much more efficient, not to mention cheaper to produce. On radiators with plastic end caps, there are gaskets between the aluminum core and the plastic tanks to seal the system and keep the fluid from leaking out. On older copper and brass radiators, the tanks were brazed (a form of welding) in order to seal the radiator.

The tanks, whether plastic or brass, each have a large hose connection, one mounted towards the top of the radiator to let the coolant in, the other mounted at the bottom of the radiator on the other tank to let the coolant back out. On the top of the radiator is an additional opening that is capped off by the radiator cap.

Another component in the radiator for machines with an automatic transmission is a separate tank mounted inside one of the tanks. Fittings connect this inner tank through steel tubes to the automatic transmission. Transmission fluid is piped through this tank inside a tank to be cooled by the coolant flowing past it before returning the transmission.

**Radiator cap**

In order to prevent the coolant from boiling, the cooling system is designed to be pressurized. Under pressure, the boiling point of the coolant is raised considerably. However, too much pressure will cause hoses and other parts to burst, so a system is needed to relieve pressure if it exceeds a certain point. The job of maintaining the pressure in the cooling system belongs to the radiator cap. The cap is designed to release pressure if it reaches the specified upper limit that the system was designed to handle. Prior to the 1970s, the cap would release this extra pressure to the pavement. Since then, a system was added to capture any released fluid and store it temporarily in a reserve tank. This fluid would then return to the cooling system after the engine cooled down. This is what is called a closed cooling system.

**Water Pump**

A water pump is a simple device that will keep the coolant moving as long as the engine is running. It is usually mounted on the front of the engine and turns whenever the engine is running.

The water pump is made up of a housing, usually made of cast iron or cast aluminum and an impeller mounted on a spinning shaft with a pulley attached to the shaft on the outside of the pump body. A seal keeps fluid from leaking out of the pump housing past the spinning shaft. The impeller uses centrifugal force to draw the coolant in from the lower radiator hose and send it under pressure into the engine block. There is a gasket to seal the water pump to the engine block and prevent the flowing coolant from leaking out where the pump is attached to the block.

**Fan**

Mounted on the back of the radiator on the side closest to the engine is one or two electric fans inside a housing that is designed to protect fingers and to direct the air flow. These fans are there to keep the air flow going through the radiator while the machine is going slow or is stopped with the engine running. If these fans stopped working, every time you came to a stop, the engine temperature would begin rising. On older systems, the fan was connected to the front of the water pump and would spin whenever the engine was running because it was driven by a fan belt instead of an electric motor. In these cases, if a driver would notice the engine begin to run hot in stop and go driving, the driver might put the machine in neutral and rev the engine to turn the fan faster which helped cool the engine. Racing the engine on a machine with a malfunctioning electric fan would only make things worse because you are producing more heat in the radiator with no fan to cool it off.

The electric fans are controlled by the computer. A temperature sensor monitors engine temperature and sends this information to the computer. The computer determines if the fan should be turned on and actuates the fan relay if additional air flow through the radiator is necessary.

If the machine has air conditioning, there is an additional radiator mounted in front of the normal radiator. This "radiator" is called the air conditioner condenser, which also needs to be cooled by the air flow entering the engine compartment. As long as the air conditioning is turned on, the system will keep the fan running, even if the engine is not running hot. This is because if there is no air flow through the air conditioning condenser, the air conditioner will not be able to cool the air entering the interior.

**Thermostat**

A thermostat is placed between the engine and the radiator to make sure that the coolant stays above a certain preset temperature. It is simply a valve that measures the temperature of the coolant and, if it is hot enough, opens to allow the coolant to flow through the radiator. If the coolant is not hot enough, the flow to the radiator is blocked and fluid is directed to a bypass system that allows the coolant to return directly back to the engine. The bypass system allows the coolant to keep moving through the engine to balance the temperature and avoid hot spots. Because flow to the radiator is blocked, the engine will reach operating temperature sooner and, on a cold day, will allow the heater to begin supplying hot air to the interior more quickly.

The heart of a thermostat is a sealed copper cup that contains wax and a metal pellet. As the thermostat heats up, the hot wax expands, pushing a piston against spring pressure to open the valve and allow coolant to circulate. The thermostat is usually located in the front, top part of the engine in a water outlet housing that also serves as the connection point for the upper radiator hose. The thermostat housing attaches to the engine, usually with two bolts and a gasket to seal it against leaks. The gasket is usually made of a heavy paper or a rubber O ring is used. In some applications, there is no gasket or rubber seal. Instead, a thin bead of special silicone sealer is squeezed from a tube to form a seal.

### Bypass System

This is a passage that allows the coolant to bypass the radiator and return directly back to the engine. Some engines use a rubber hose, or a fixed steel tube. In other engines, there is a cast in passage built into the water pump or front housing. In any case, when the thermostat is closed, coolant is directed to this bypass and channeled back to the water pump, which sends the coolant back into the engine without being cooled by the radiator.

### Antifreeze

The coolant that courses through the engine and associated plumbing must be able to withstand temperatures well below zero without freezing. It must also be able to handle engine temperatures in excess of 250 degrees without boiling. A tall order for any fluid, but that is not all. The fluid must also contain rust inhibiters and a lubricant.

The coolant in today's machines is a mixture of ethylene glycol (antifreeze) and water. The recommended ratio is fifty-fifty. In other words, one part antifreeze and one part water. This is the minimum recommended for use in automobile engines. Less antifreeze and the boiling point would be too low. In certain climates where the temperatures can go well below zero, it is permissible to have as much as 75 percent antifreeze and 25 percent water, but no more than that. Pure antifreeze will not work properly and can cause a boil over.

Antifreeze is poisonous and should be kept away from people and animals, especially dogs and cats, who are attracted by the sweet taste. Ethylene glycol, if ingested, will form calcium oxalate crystals in the kidneys which can cause acute renal failure and death.

## Lubricating System

Lubrication is perhaps the most important single factor in the successful operation of diesel engines. Consequently, too much emphasis cannot be placed upon the importance of the lubricating oil system and lubrication in general. It is not only important that the proper type of oil be used, but it must be supplied to the engine in the proper quantities, at the proper temperature, and provisions must be made to remove any impurities as they enter the system. In general, the basic requirements that a lubricating system must meet to perform its functions satisfactorily are:

1. An effective lubricating system must correctly distribute a proper supply of oil to all bearing surfaces.

2. It must supply sufficient oil for cooling purposes to all parts requiring oil cooling.

3. The system must provide tanks to collect the oil that has been used for lubrication and cooling, so that it can be recirculated throughout the system.

4. The system must include coolers to maintain the oil temperature within the most efficient operating temperature range.

5. In order to exclude dirt and water from the working parts of the engine, filters and strainers

must be included in the system to clean the oil as it circulates.

6. Adequate facilities must be provided on the ship for storing the required quantity of lubricating oil necessary for extensive operation and for transferring this oil to the engine lubricating systems as needed.

**The Operation of Engine Lubricating Oil System** (shown as Figure 3-3)

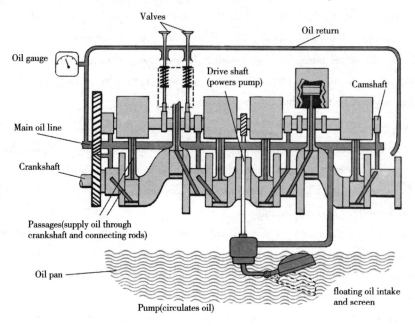

Figure 3-3   Lubricating System

Oil is drawn from the sump tank by the attached lubricating oil pump. The discharge from this pump passes through the lubricating oil strainer. Between the discharge side of the pump and the strainer is a relief valve built integral with the pump. From the strainer the oil is carried to the lubricating oil cooler and thence to the engine main lubricating oil headers. The strainer is always placed forward of the cooler in the system because, if the temperature of the lubricating oil is higher, its filtering efficiency will be greater and the power necessary to force the oil through the strainer will be less.

In most installations the lubricating oil goes from the main lube oil headers to the engine main bearings and thence to the connecting rod bearings. The oil then passes through a drilled hole in the connecting rod up to the piston pin bearing which it lubricates and sprays out onto the under surface of the piston crown. Next, it drains down into the oil drain pan, carrying away from the piston much of the heat caused by combustion. From the oil pan, the oil drains to the engine sump tank from which it is recirculated.

Between the oil pan and the sump tank, screens and basket type strainers may be inserted to prevent small metallic particles from draining down into the sump tank.

The lubricating oil pumps are designed to deliver considerably more oil than is normally required to pass through the engines. This insures sufficient lubrication when changes in the rate of oil flow occur because of cold starting, changes in speed, changes in viscosity of the oil due to heat, or increases in bearing clearances.

Pressure gages are placed in the system to indicate the pressures of the lubricating oil entering the strainer, leaving the strainer, and entering the engine. Through a change in pressure readings at these gages, troubles such as air binding of pumps, broken supply lines, or dirty strainers may be localized and remedied.

The lubricating oil is cooled by fresh or salt water circulating through an oil cooler. The pressure of the lubricating oil is higher than the pressure of the water so that, in the event of a leak, water cannot enter the oil system.

## Word List

1. maintain [meinˈtein]　　　　　　　　vt. 保持,维持;保养
2. Fahrenheit [ˈfærənˌhaɪt]　　　　　　n. 华氏温度计
3. suffer [ˈsʌfə]　　　　　　　　　　　vi. 受痛苦;受损害
　　　　　　　　　　　　　　　　　　vt. 忍受;容忍;容许;遭受
4. thermostat [ˈθɜːməˌstæt]　　　　　　n. 恒温(调节)器
5. coolant [ˈkuːlənt]　　　　　　　　　n. 冷冻剂,冷却液,散热剂
6. radiator [ˈreɪdiːˌeɪtə]　　　　　　　n. 散热器;(汽车发动机的)冷却器
7. plumbing [ˈplʌmɪŋ]　　　　　　　　n. 水管装置,水暖设备
8. flatten [ˈflætn]　　　　　　　　　　vt. & vi. 变平,使(某物)变平;打倒
9. undergo [ˌʌndəˈgəu]　　　　　　　　vt. 经历,经验;遭受,承受
10. capture [ˈkæptʃə]　　　　　　　　　vt. 俘获;夺取;夺得;引起
　　　　　　　　　　　　　　　　　　n. 捕获,占领;捕获物
11. aluminum [əˈluːmənəm]　　　　　　n. 铝
12. strip [strip]　　　　　　　　　　　vi. 剥除
　　　　　　　　　　　　　　　　　　vt. 除去,剥去;清除,拆除
　　　　　　　　　　　　　　　　　　n. 长条,条板
13. zigzag [ˈzigzæg]　　　　　　　　　adj. (指线条、小径等)之字形的,Z字形的
　　　　　　　　　　　　　　　　　　n. 锯齿形的线条、小径等
　　　　　　　　　　　　　　　　　　vi. 弯弯曲曲地走路,曲折地前进
14. fin [fin]　　　　　　　　　　　　　n. 散热片
15. horizontal [ˌhɔriˈzɔntəl]　　　　　adj. 水平的
16. brass [brɑːs]　　　　　　　　　　　n. 黄铜
17. braze [breiz]　　　　　　　　　　　vt. 铜焊
18. spin [spin]　　　　　　　　　　　　vi. 快速旋转
19. impeller [imˈpelə]　　　　　　　　　n. 叶轮
20. gasket [ˈgæskit]　　　　　　　　　　n. 束帆索,垫圈,衬垫
21. neutral [ˈnjuːtrəl]　　　　　　　　　n. (汽车或其他机器的)空挡位置
22. rev [rev]　　　　　　　　　　　　　n. 发动机的旋转
　　　　　　　　　　　　　　　　　　vt. & vi. (使)加速
23. climate [ˈklaimit]　　　　　　　　　n. 气候
24. actuate [ˈæktʃuːˌeit]　　　　　　　　vt. 使动作;开动;驱使;激励

25. rust [rʌst]     n. 铁锈
                         vt. & vi. (使)生锈
26. inhibiter [ɪnˈhɪbɪtə]     n. 缓蚀剂
27. antifreeze [ˈæntɪˌfriːz]     n. 防冻剂
28. ingest [ɪnˈdʒest]     vt. 咽下
29. kidney [ˈkɪdni]     n. 肾，肾脏
30. poisonous [ˈpɔɪzənəs]     adj. 有毒的
31. withstand [wɪðˈstænd]     vt. 经受，承受，禁得起；反抗
                         vi. 反抗；耐得住，禁得起
32. recommend [ˌrekəˈmend]     vt. 推荐；劝告；托付
                         vi. 推荐；建议
33. consequently [ˈkɔnsikwəntli]     adv. 所以，因此
34. emphasis [ˈemfəsis]     n. 强调；着重
35. impurity [ɪmˈpjʊərɪtiː]     n. 污点，污染；掺杂，不纯
36. satisfactorily [ˌsætɪsˈfæktərɪlɪ]     adv. 令人满意地；心安理得地
37. strainer [ˈstreɪnə]     n. 滤器，滤盆，滤网
38. discharge [disˈtʃɑːdʒ]     vt. & vi. 放出；流出；开枪；发射
                         n. (气体、液体如水从管子里)流出
39. integral [ˈintigrəl]     adj. 完整的

## Proper Names

1. keep away from     (使)不接近；避开
2. in excess of     多于，超出
3. ethylene glycol     乙二醇
4. not to mention     更不用说
5. heater core     暖气风箱
6. air conditioning     空气调节装置
7. in the event of     万一，倘若
8. prior to     在……之前
9. a closed cooling system     闭路冷却系统
10. relief valve     安全阀
11. bearing clearance     轴承间隙

## Notes

①The cooling system is made up of the passages inside the engine block and heads, a water pump to circulate the coolant, a thermostat to control the temperature of the coolant, a radiator to cool the coolant, a radiator cap to control the pressure in the system, and some plumbing consisting of interconnecting hoses to transfer the coolant from the engine to radiator and also to the machine's heater system where hot coolant is used to warm up the machine's interior on a cold day.

(强制循环式)水冷却系由发动机内的部件组成：冷却水套、使冷却剂循环的水泵、控制冷

却剂的恒温器、使冷却剂冷却的散热器、控制系统内压力的散热器盖和一些包含相互连接的软管的水管装置。这些装置将冷却剂从发动机转移到散热器,也转移到机器加热系统,在这里,在寒冷的日子,热冷却剂被用来给机器内部加热。

## Exercises

**1. Vocabulary link**

| | |
|---|---|
| thermostat | 空气调节装置 |
| radiator | 润滑系统 |
| air conditioning | 恒温器 |
| cooling system | 散热器 |
| lubricating system | 冷却系统 |

**2. Fill in the blanks with the word or phrase that correctly completes the meaning.**

There are two types of cooling systems found on machines: (　　　) and (　　　).

# Practical Reading

## Lubricating Oil

### 润滑油

Lubricating oil in a diesel engine is used for the following purposes:
- To prevent metal-to-metal contact between moving parts.
- To aid in engine cooling.
- To form a seal between the piston rings and the cylinder wall.
- To aid in keeping the inside of cylinder walls free of sludge and lacquer.

A direct metal-to-metal moving contact has an action that is comparable to a filing action. This filing action is due to minute irregularities in the surfaces, and its harshness depends upon the force of the contacting surfaces as well as on the relative hardness of the materials used. Lubricating oil is used to fill these minute irregularities and to form a film seal between the sliding surfaces, thereby preventing high friction losses, rapid engine wear, and many operating difficulties. Lack of this oil film seal results in seized, or frozen pistons, wiped bearings, and stuck piston rings. The high-pressures of air and fuel in diesel engines can cause blow-by of exhaust gases between the piston rings and cylinder liner unless lubricating oil forms a seal between these parts.

Lubricating oil is used to assist in cooling by transferring or carrying away heat from localized hot spots in the engine. Heat is carried away from bearings, tops of the pistons, and other engine parts by the lubricating oil. It is the volume of lubricating oil being circulated that makes cooling of an engine possible. For example, under average conditions, an 8-inch by 10-inch cylinder requires about 24 drops of oil per minute for lubrication of the cylinder wall. About 30 drops of oil per minute normally will lubricate a large bearing when the engine is running at high speed. Yet some engines circulate as much as 40 gallons of lubricating oil per minute. This illustrates how much of the lubricating oil is used for cooling purposes.

Lubricating oil that is used to form a seal between piston rings and cylinder walls or on any other rubbing or sliding surface must meet the following requirements:

- The oil film must be of a sufficient thickness and strength, and must be maintained under all conditions of operation. In order to maintain a strong oil film or body under varying temperature conditions, a lubricating oil must have stability. Stability of the oil should be such that a proper oil film is maintained throughout the entire operating temperature range of the engine. Such a film will insure sufficient oiliness or film strength between the piston and cylinder walls so that partly burned fuel and exhaust gases cannot get by the piston rings to form sludge.
- The oil temperature attained during operation must be limited.
- Under normal changing temperature conditions the oil must remain stable.
- The oil must not have a corrosive action on metallic surfaces.

To insure satisfactory performance a lubricating oil must have certain physical properties which are determined by various types of tests. These tests give some indication of how the oil may perform in practice. Some of the tests are as follows:

1. Viscosity. The viscosity of the oil is a measure of its internal friction of the fluid. Viscosity is generally considered to be the most important property of a lubricating oil since friction, wear, and oil consumption are more or less dependent on this characteristic.

2. Pour point. The lowest temperature at which the oil will barely pour from a container is the pour point. High pour point lubricating oil usually causes difficulty in starting in cold weather due to the inability of the lubricating oil pump to pump oil through the lubricating system.

3. Carbon residue. The amount of carbon left after the volatile matter in lubricating oil has been evaporated is known as the carbon residue of the oil. The carbon residue test gives an indication of the amount of carbon that may be deposited in an engine. Excessive carbon in an engine leads to operating difficulties.

4. Flash point. The lowest temperature at which the vapors of a heated oil will flash is the flash point of the oil. The flash point of an oil is the fire hazard measure used in determining storage dangers. Practically all lubricating oils have flash points that are high enough to eliminate the fire hazard during storage in submarine, tender, or base stowage facilities.

5. Corrosion. The tendency of the oil to corrode the engine parts is known as the corrosive quality of the lubricating oil. The appearance of a strip of sheet copper immersed in oil at 212 degrees F for 3 hours formerly was thought to indicate the corrosive tendency of an oil. This test, however, is not necessarily a criterion of the corrosive tendency of the newer compounded oils, some of which do darken the copper strip but are not corrosive in service. Corrosive oil has a tendency to eat away the soft bearing metals, resulting in serious damage to the bearing.

6. Water and sediment. Water and sediment in a lubricating oil normally are the result of improper handling and stowage. Lubricating oil should be free of water and sediment after leaving the purifier and on arriving at the engine.

7. Ash. The ash content of an oil is a measure of the amount of noncombustible material present that would cause abrasion or scoring of moving parts.

## Word List

1. sludge [slʌdʒ]      n. 泥浆,烂泥;沉淀物;泥状雪
     v. 清除污泥
2. lacquer ['lækə]      n. 漆,天然漆;漆器
     vt. 涂漆于;使…表面或外观光滑
3. minute [mai'nju:t]      adj. 极小的;微不足道的
4. irregularities [ˌiregə'læriti:z]      n. 不规则
5. filing ['failiŋ]      n. 整理成档案,文件归档,锉
     v. 把…归档;用锉锉
6. harshness ['hɑ:ʃnis]      n. 粗糙的事物,严肃,刺耳
7. corrosive [kə'rəusiv]      adj. 腐蚀性的;侵蚀性的
8. indication [ˌindi'keiʃən]      n. 指示;象征
9. criterion [krai'tiəriən]      n. (批评、判断等的)标准,准则;规范
10. corrosion [kə'rəuʃən]      n. 腐蚀,侵蚀,锈蚀

## Proper Names

1. in honor of      为了向…表示敬意
2. lawn mowers      草坪割草机
3. due to      由于
4. blow-by      窜气

## 参考答案

**1. Vocabulary link**

| | |
|---|---|
| thermostat | 恒温器 |
| radiator | 散热器 |
| air conditioning | 空气调节装置 |
| cooling system | 冷却系统 |
| lubricating system | 润滑系统 |

**2. Fill in the blanks with the word or phrase that correctly completes the meaning.**

There are two types of cooling systems found on machines: liquid cooled and air cooled.

# 项目 4

# 传动系统的认识

**学习目标**

完成本项目学习任务后,你应当能:

1. 认识关于传动系统的专业术语,熟悉传动系统的工作过程及发展状况;
2. 基于所学专业知识,借助专业词典的帮助,能无障碍地查阅与传动系统相关的英语资料;
3. 正确完成课后练习。

**任务描述**

通过本文学习,完成相关单词、词汇、特殊语句的学习,认识传动系统的分类、组成,及各自工作原理。强化相关专业英文资料的阅读能力。

**引导问题**

参照以下图片,对比离合器与液力变矩器的异同。

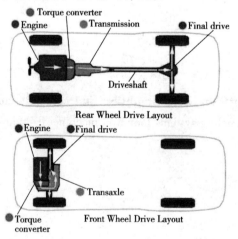

**学 时**

8 学时

# 学习引导

本学习任务沿着以下脉络进行学习：

复习相关专业知识 → 学习单词和语法 → 通读全文 → 完成课后练习 → 课后阅读

# Project 4　Acquaintance with Transmission System

**Transmission**

To understand the basic idea behind a standard transmission, the diagram below shows a very simple two-speed transmission in neutral.

Let's look at each of the parts in this diagram to understand how they fit together (shown as Figure 4-1):

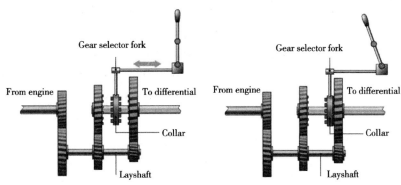

Figure 4-1　A Simple Transmission

• The left shaft comes from the engine through the clutch. The left shaft and its gear are connected as a single unit. (The clutch is a device that lets you connect and disconnect the engine and the transmission. When you push in the clutch pedal, the engine and the transmission are disconnected so the engine can run even if the car is standing still. When you release the clutch pedal, the engine and the green shaft are directly connected to one another. The left shaft and its gear turn at the same speed as the engine.)

• The middle shaft and gears are called the layshaft. These are also connected as a single piece, so all of the gears on the layshaft and the layshaft itself spin as one unit. The left shaft and the middle shaft are directly connected through their meshed gears so that if the left shaft is spinning, so is the middle shaft. In this way, the layshaft receives its power directly from the engine whenever the clutch is engaged.

• The right shaft is a splined shaft that connects directly to the drive shaft through the differential to the drive wheels of the machine. If the wheels are spinning, the right shaft is spinning. And its gears ride on bearings, so they spin on the right shaft. If the engine is off but the car is coasting, the right shaft can turn while its gears and the layshaft are motionless.

• The purpose of the collar is to connect one of the two gears to the right drive shaft. The collar is connected, through the splines, directly to the right shaft and spins with the right shaft. However, the collar can slide left or right along the right shaft to engage either of the two gears. Teeth on the collar, called dog teeth, fit into holes on the sides of the blue gears to engage them.

Now, let's see what happens when you shift into first gear (shown as Figure 4-1).

In this picture, the left shaft from the engine turns the layshaft, which turns the driven gear of the right shaft on the right. This gear transmits its energy through the collar to drive the right drive shaft. Meanwhile, the another driven gear on the left is turning, but it is freewheeling on its bearing so it has no effect on the right shaft.

When the collar is between the two gears (as shown in the first figure), the transmission is in neutral. Both of the driven gears freewheel on the right shaft at the different rates controlled by their ratios to the layshaft.

## Clutches

Clutches are useful in engineering machines that have two rotating shafts. You need a clutch because the engine spins all the time, but the machine's wheels do not. In order for a machine to stop without killing the engine, the wheels need to be disconnected from the engine somehow. In these machines, one of the shafts is typically driven by a motor or pulley, and the other shaft drives another device. In a drill, for instance, one shaft is driven by a motor and the other drives a drill chuck. The clutch connects the two shafts so that they can either be locked together and spin at the same speed, or be decoupled and spin at different speeds. [①] The clutch allows us to smoothly engage a spinning engine to a non-spinning transmission by controlling the slippage between them.

To understand how a clutch works, it helps to know a little bit about friction, which is a measure of how hard it is to slide one object over another. Friction is caused by the peaks and valleys that are part of every surface—even very smooth surfaces still have microscopic peaks and valleys. The larger these peaks and valleys are, the harder it is to slide the object.

A clutch works because of friction between a clutch plate and a flywheel. We'll look at how these parts work together in the next section.

In a machine's clutch, a flywheel connects to the engine, and a clutch plate connects to the transmission. When your foot is off the pedal, the springs push the pressure plate against the clutch disc, which in turn presses against the flywheel. This locks the engine to the transmission input shaft, causing them to spin at the same speed (shown as Figure 4-2).

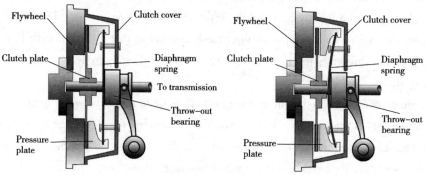

Figure 4-2  Engaged and Disengaged Clutch

The amount of force the clutch can hold depends on the friction between the clutch plate and the flywheel, and how much force the spring puts on the pressure plate. The friction force in the clutch works just like the blocks described in the friction section of How Brakes Work, except that the spring presses on the clutch plate instead of weight pressing the block into the ground.

When the clutch pedal is pressed (shown as Figure 4-2), a cable or hydraulic piston pushes on the release fork, which presses the throw-out bearing against the middle of the diaphragm spring. As the middle of the diaphragm spring is pushed in, a series of pins near the outside of the spring causes the spring to pull the pressure plate away from the clutch disc. This releases the clutch from the spinning engine.

Note the springs in the clutch plate. These springs help to isolate the transmission from the shock of the clutch engaging.

This design usually works pretty well, but it does have a few drawbacks. We'll look at common clutch problems in the following sections.

**Common Problems**

From the 1950s to the 1970s, you could count on getting between 50,000 and 70,000 miles from your clutch. Clutches can now last for more than 80,000 miles if you use them gently and maintain them well. If not cared for, clutches can start to break down at 35,000 miles. Vehicles that are consistently overloaded or that frequently tow heavy loads can also have problems with relatively new clutches.

**Slipping**

The most common problem with clutches is that the friction material on the disc wears out. The friction material on a clutch disc is very similar to the friction material on the pads of a disc brake or the shoes of a drum brake—after a while, it wears away. [2]When most or all of the friction material is gone, the clutch will start to slip, and eventually it won't transmit any power from the engine to the wheels.

The clutch only wears while the clutch disc and the flywheel are spinning at different speeds. When they are locked together, the friction material is held tightly against the flywheel, and they spin in sync. It's only when the clutch disc is slipping against the flywheel that wearing occurs. So, if you are the type of driver who slips the clutch a lot, you'll wear out your clutch a lot faster.

**Sticking**

Sometimes the problem is not with slipping, but with sticking. If your clutch won't release properly, it will continue to turn the input shaft. This can cause grinding, or completely prevent your machine from going into gear. Some common reasons a clutch may stick are:

• Broken or stretched clutch cable-The cable needs the right amount of tension to push and pull effectively.

• Leaky or defective slave and/or master clutch cylinders-Leaks keep the cylinders from building the necessary amount of pressure.

• Air in the hydraulic line-Air affects the hydraulics by taking up space the fluid needs to build pressure.

• Misadjusted linkage-When your foot hits the pedal, the linkage transmits the wrong amount of force.

- Mismatched clutch components-Not all aftermarket parts work with your clutch.

**"Hard" clutch**

A "hard" clutch is also a common problem. All clutches require some amount of force to depress fully. If you have to press hard on the pedal, there may be something wrong. Sticking or binding in the pedal linkage, cable, cross shaft, or pivot ball are common causes. Sometimes a blockage or worn seals in the hydraulic system can also cause a hard clutch.

Another problem associated with clutches is a worn throw-out bearing, sometimes called a clutch release bearing. This bearing applies force to the fingers of the spinning pressure plate to release the clutch. If you hear a rumbling sound when the clutch engages, you might have a problem with the throw-out bearing.

**Differentials**

The differential has three jobs:

- To aim the engine power at the wheels.
- To act as the final gear reduction in the machine, slowing the rotational speed of the transmission one final time before it hits the wheels.
- To transmit the power to the wheels while allowing them to rotate at different speeds (This is the one that earned the differential its name).

The differential is a gear assembly in a motor machine which allows the propeller shaft to drive shaft, to turn the machine wheels at different speeds when the machine is going around a curve. When a machine goes around a curve, the wheel on the inside of the curve travels less distance than the other, and so must turn more slowly, for safety in handling and to keep tyre wear to a minimum. A four wheel drive machine has two differentials. For maximum traction, a four wheel drive machine has been designed with three differentials, separating the front wheels, the rear wheels and the front from the rear, allowing each wheel to turn at its own speed under power[3] (shown as Figure 4-3). The only car which does not have a differential is the DAF car, built in Holland, which has a belt drive system allowing slippage of the belt on the pulleys.

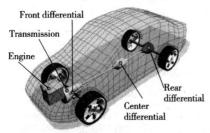

Figure 4-3  All-wheel Drive

The differential is encased in a casting, which is located on most machines (have rear wheel drive) in the middle of the rear axles between the wheels. (It is sometimes called the "cabbage head" because of its bulbous appearance.) The drive shaft enters the casting in the front and one axle enters at each side. A pinion gear, which is splined into the end of the drive shaft, turns a beveled crown gear which is fastened onto the end of one of the axles. An assembly of four small beveled gears (two pinions and two star gears) is bolted to the crown gear and turns with it.[4] The other axle is driven by the small pinion gear opposite the crown gear. The assembly drives both axles at the same speed when the machine is being driven in a straight line, but allows the axle opposite the crown gear to turn slower or faster, as required[5] (shown as Figure 4-4).

Some units are designed to give a limited-slip or slip-lock differential, to equalize power between the wheels on a slippery or a soft road surface, providing safe handling and minimizing the likelihood of getting stuck snow or soft earth.

The gear ratio (ratio of the number of teeth on one gear to the number of teeth on the other) between the crown gear and the pinion gear is one of the factors that determine the performance characteristics of the machine, such as acceleration and top speed. ⑥

Early machines had pinion and crown gears with straight teeth on them, which resulted in noisy

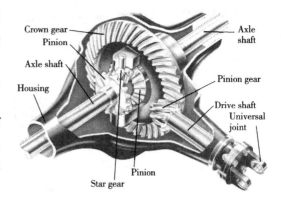

Figure 4-4  Differentials

operation of the differential and allowed play in the gear teeth, causing undue wear. Today the pinion and crown gears are helical gears, which means that the toothed surfaces are beveled and the teeth themselves are curved. This design eliminates play between the teeth, because as the gears spin together one tooth is in full contact before the previous tooth leaves. ⑦ A properly constructed differential should last the life of the machine without any maintenance at all.

In order to produce a particularly quiet differential, the pinion and crown gears are lapped together in a lapping machine which duplicates the operating conditions of the completed differential. ⑧ After lapping, the two gears are kept together as a set. They are inspected together in a machine in a quiet room, which determines the exact thickness of shims (sheet metal discs used to ensure a close fit) required in the assembly to ensure quiet operation; then they go to the differential assembly line. All the gears in the system are installed against roller bearings, the proper shimming is installed; then the unit is test-run, filled with a heavy oil and sealed. Quiet operation of the differential is essential in a machine with unit-body construction, as opposed to a separate body bolted to a frame, because noise from the differential will be transmitted by the body itself.

## Power Steering

You might be surprised to learn that when you turn your machine, your front wheels are not pointing in the same direction (shown as Figure 4-5).

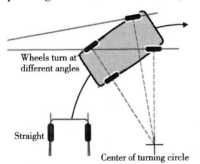

Figure 4-5  Steering-running

For a machine to turn smoothly, each wheel must follow a different circle. Since the inside wheel is following a circle with a smaller radius, it is actually making a tighter turn than the outside wheel. If you draw a line perpendicular to each wheel, the lines will intersect at the center point of the turn. The geometry of the steering linkage makes the inside wheel turn more than the outside wheel (shown as Figure 4-6).

### Components

There are a couple of key components in power steering in addition to the rack-and-pinion or recirculating-ball mechanism which are the most common types of steering gears: pump and rotary valve (shown as Figure 4-7).

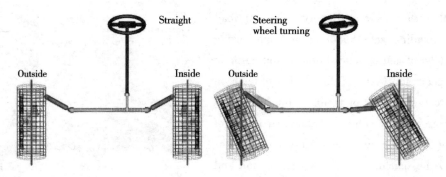

Figure 4-6    How Steering Works

**Rack-and-pinion Steering**

Rack-and-pinion steering is quickly becoming the most common type of steering on machines. It is actually a pretty simple mechanism. A rack-and-pinion gear set is enclosed in a metal tube, with each end of the rack protruding from the tube. ⑨A rod, called a tie rod, connects to each end of the rack.

The pinion gear is attached to the steering shaft. When you turn the steering wheel, the gear spins, moving the rack. The tie rod at each end of the rack connects to the steering arm on the spindle(shown as Figure 4-8).

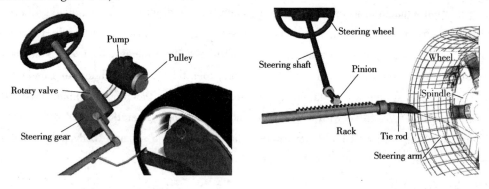

Figure 4-7    Steering Parts          Figure 4-8    Steering-rack

The rack-and-pinion gear set does two things:

• It converts the rotational motion of the steering wheel into the linear motion needed to turn the wheels.

• It provides a gear reduction, making it easier to turn the wheels.

On most machines, it takes three to four complete revolutions of the steering wheel to make the wheels turn from lock to lock (from far left to far right).

The steering ratio is the ratio of how far you turn the steering wheel to how far the wheels turn. For instance, if one complete revolution (360 degrees) of the steering wheel results in the wheels of the car turning 20 degrees, then the steering ratio is 360 divided by 20, or 18:1. A higher ratio means that you have to turn the steering wheel more to get the wheels to turn a given distance. However, less effort is required because of the higher gear ratio.

When the rack-and-pinion is in a power-steering system, the rack has a slightly different design.

Part of the rack contains a cylinder with a piston in the middle. The piston is connected to the rack. There are two fluid ports, one on either side of the piston. Supplying higher-pressure fluid to one side of the piston forces the piston to move, which in turn moves the rack, providing the power assist (shown as Figure 4-9).

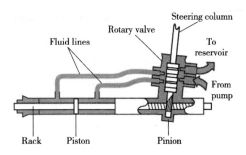

Figure 4-9　Steering-power-rack

### Recirculating-ball Steering

The linkage that turns the wheels is slightly different than on a rack-and-pinion system.

The recirculating-ball steering gear contains a worm gear. You can image the gear in two parts. The first part is a block of metal with a threaded hole in it. This block has gear teeth cut into the outside of it, which engage a gear that moves the pitman arm. The steering wheel connects to a threaded rod, similar to a bolt, that sticks into the hole in the block. When the steering wheel turns, it turns the bolt. Instead of twisting further into the block the way a regular bolt would, this bolt is held fixed so that when it spins, it moves the block, which moves the gear that turns the wheels (shown as Figure 4-10).

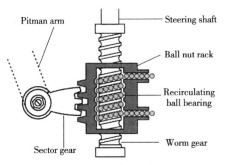 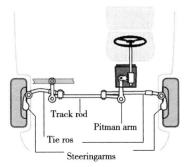

Figure 4-10　Steering-ball

Instead of the bolt directly engaging the threads in the block, all of the threads are filled with ball bearings that recirculate through the gear as it turns. The balls actually serve two purposes: First, they reduce friction and wear in the gear; second, they reduce slop in the gear. ⑩Slop would be felt when you change the direction of the steering wheel—without the balls in the steering gear, the teeth would come out of contact with each other for a moment, making the steering wheel feel loose.

Power steering in a recirculating-ball system works similarly to a rack-and-pinion system. Assist is provided by supplying higher-pressure fluid to one side of the block.

### Pump

The hydraulic power for the steering is provided by a rotary-vane pump. This pump is driven by the engine via a belt and pulley. It contains a set of retractable vanes that spin inside an oval chamber (shown as Figure 4-11).

As the vanes spin, they pull hydraulic fluid from

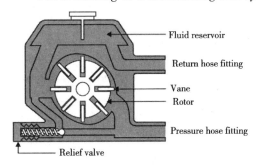

Figure 4-11　Steering-pump-diagram

the return line at low pressure and force it into the outlet at high pressure. The amount of flow provided by the pump depends on the engine speed. The pump must be designed to provide adequate flow when the engine is idling. As a result, the pump moves much more fluid than necessary when the engine is running at faster speeds. The pump contains a pressure-relief valve to make sure that the pressure does not get too high, especially at high engine speeds when so much fluid is being pumped.

### Rotary Valve

A power-steering system should assist the driver only when he is exerting force on the steering wheel (such as when starting a turn). When the driver is not exerting force (such as when driving in a straight line), the system shouldn't provide any assist. The device that senses the force on the steering wheel is called the rotary valve.

The key to the rotary valve is a torsion bar. The torsion bar is a thin rod of metal that twists when torque is applied to it. The top of the bar is connected to the steering wheel, and the bottom of the bar is connected to the pinion or worm gear (which turns the wheels), so the amount of torque in the torsion bar is equal to the amount of torque the driver is using to turn the wheels. The more torque the driver uses to turn the wheels, the more the bar twists.

### Brakes

What do brakes do? The simple answer: they slow you down.

The complex answer: brakes are designed to slow down your vehicle but probably not by the means that you think. The common misconception is that brakes squeeze against a drum or disc, and the pressure of the squeezing action is what slows you down. This in fact is only part of the equation. Brakes are essentially a mechanism to change energy types. When you're traveling at speed, your vehicle has kinetic energy. When you apply the brakes, the pads or shoes that press against the brake drum or rotor convert that energy into thermal energy via friction. The cooling of the brakes dissipates the heat and the vehicle slows down. It's the First Law of Thermodynamics, sometimes known as the law of conservation of energy. This states that energy cannot be created nor destroyed, it can only be converted from one form to another. In the case of brakes, it is converted from kinetic energy to thermal energy.

When you depress your brake pedal, your car transmits the force from your foot to its brakes through a fluid. Since the actual brakes require a much greater force than you could apply with your leg, your car must also multiply the force of your foot. It does this in two ways:

- Mechanical advantage (leverage).
- Hydraulic force multiplication.

You can see that the distance from the pedal to the pivot is four times the distance from the cylinder to the pivot, so the force at the pedal will be increased by a factor of four before it is transmitted to the cylinder.

You can also see that the diameter of the brake cylinder is three times the diameter of the pedal cylinder. This further multiplies the force by nine. All together, this system increases the force of your foot by a factor of 36. If you put 10 pounds of force on the pedal, 360 pounds (162kg) will be generated at the wheel squeezing the brake pads (shown as Figure 4-12).

### Disc Brakes

The main components of a disc brake are:
- The brake pads.
- The caliper, which contains a piston.
- The rotor, which is mounted to the hub.

The disc brake is a lot like the brakes on a bicycle. Bicycle brakes have a caliper, which squeezes the brake pads against the wheel. In a disc brake, the brake pads squeeze the rotor instead of the wheel, and the force is transmitted hydraulically instead of through a cable. Friction between the pads and the disc slows the disc down (shown as Figure 4-13).

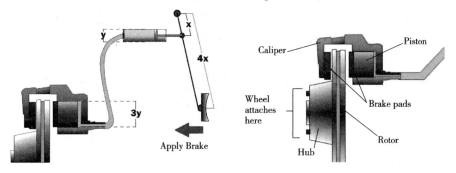

Figure 4-12　A Simple Brake System　　　　Figure 4-13　Disc-brakes

A moving car has a certain amount of kinetic energy, and the brakes have to remove this energy from the car in order to stop it. How do the brakes do this? Each time you stop your car, your brakes convert the kinetic energy to heat generated by the friction between the pads and the disc. Most car disc brakes are vented.

Vented disc brakes have a set of vanes, between the two sides of the disc, that pumps air through the disc to provide cooling

### Drum Brakes

Drum brakes work on the same principle as disc brakes: Shoes press against a spinning surface. In this system, that surface is called a drum (shown as Figure 4-14).

Many machines have drum brakes on the rear wheels and disc brakes on the front. Drum brakes have more parts than disc brakes and are harder to service, but they are less expensive to manufacture, and they easily incorporate an emergency brake mechanism.

The drum brake may look complicated, and it can be pretty intimidating when you open one up. Let's break it down and explain what each piece does.

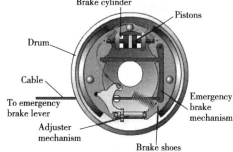

Figure 4-14　Drum-brakes

Like the disc brake, the drum brake has two brake shoes and a piston. But the drum brake also has an adjuster mechanism, an emergency brake mechanism and lots of springs.

When you hit the brake pedal, the piston pushes the brake shoes against the drum. That's pretty straightforward, but why do we need all of those springs? This is where it gets a little more complicated. Many drum brakes are self-actuating. Figure 4-14 shows that as the brake shoes contact the drum, there is a kind of wedging action, which has the effect of pressing the shoes into the drum with more force. The extra braking force provided by the wedging action allows drum brakes to use a smaller piston than disc brakes. But, because of the wedging action, the shoes must be pulled away from the drum when the brakes are released. This is the reason for some of the springs. Other springs help hold the brake shoes in place and return the adjuster arm after it actuates.

## Word List

1. collar ['kɔlə]　　　　　　　　　　n.(管子或机器部件的)圈
2. coast [kəust]　　　　　　　　　　vi.(尤指不用动力向山坡下)滑行
3. spin [spin]　　　　　　　　　　　vi. 快速旋转；眩晕
　　　　　　　　　　　　　　　　　　n. 旋转的行为；快速的旋运动；眩晕；疾驰
4. freewheel ['fri:'hwi:l, -'wi:l]　　 n. 自由飞轮
　　　　　　　　　　　　　　　　　　vi. 轻快地行动,凭惯性前进
5. pulley ['puli]　　　　　　　　　　n. 滑轮(组),滑车；皮带轮
　　　　　　　　　　　　　　　　　　v. 用滑轮升起,用滑车推动；给……装滑车
6. chuck [tʃʌk]　　　　　　　　　　n.(钻机等的)卡盘,夹盘
7. decouple [di'kʌpl]　　　　　　　v. 使机构)分离；(使)脱离；(使)互不相干
8. slide [slaid]　　　　　　　　　　vi. 滑落；下跌；打滑；[棒球]滑垒
　　　　　　　　　　　　　　　　　　vt. 衰落(成)；逐渐降低；使悄悄转动
9. microscopic [,maikrə'skɔpik]　　adj. 显微镜的；微小的
10. transmission [trænz'miʃən]　　n.(汽车等的)传动装置,变速器
11. isolate ['aisəleit]　　　　　　　vt. 使隔离,使孤立；[化]使离析；
　　　　　　　　　　　　　　　　　　vi. 隔离,孤立
12. tow [təu]　　　　　　　　　　　vt. 拖,拉；牵引
13. sync [siŋk]　　　　　　　　　　n. 同时,同步
14. differential [,difə'renʃəl]　　　n.[机]差速器
15. propeller [prə'pelə]　　　　　　n. 螺旋桨,推进器
16. curve [kə:v]　　　　　　　　　n. 弧线,曲线；
　　　　　　　　　　　　　　　　　　vt. 使弯曲；使成曲线；使成弧形
　　　　　　　　　　　　　　　　　　vi. 弯曲；弯成曲线；沿曲线行进
　　　　　　　　　　　　　　　　　　adj. 弯曲的；曲线形的
17. tyre ['taiə]　　　　　　　　　　n. 轮胎
18. pulley ['puli]　　　　　　　　　n. 滑轮(组),滑车；皮带轮
19. encase [en'keis]　　　　　　　vt. 包装；围绕；把……装箱
20. casting ['kæstiŋ]　　　　　　　n. 铸造,铸件；
　　　　　　　　　　　　　　　　　　v. 扔掉(cast 的现在分词)；铸造
21. cabbage ['kæbidʒ]　　　　　　n. 甘蓝(洋白菜、卷心菜)
22. bulbous ['bʌlbəs]　　　　　　　adj. 球根的,球根状的,球根长成的
23. pinion ['pinjən]　　　　　　　　n.〈术〉小齿轮

| | | |
|---|---|---|
| 24. spline [splain] | | vt. 用花键联接,开键槽 |
| 25. bevel ['bevəl] | | n. 斜边和斜面;斜角规 |
| | | vt. 把(某物)切成或磨成斜边或斜角 |
| 26. bolt [bəult] | | n. 螺栓 |
| | | vt. (把门、窗等)闩上 |
| | | vi. (门窗等)闩上,拴住;冲出,跳出 |
| 27. equalize ['iːkwəlaiz] | | vt. & vi. 使相等;补偿;使均衡;打成平局 |
| 28. stuck [stʌk] | | adj. 动不了的;被卡住的;被……缠住的 |
| 29. undue [ʌn'duː, -'djuː] | | adj. 过度的,过分的;不适当的 |
| 30. helical ['helikəl] | | adj. 螺旋状的 |
| 31. lap [læp] | | vt. 磨亮,磨平 |
| 32. duplicate ['djuːplikit] | | vt. 复制,复写;重演,重复 |
| 33. inspect [in'spekt] | | vt. 检查,检验;视察 |
| | | vi. 进行检查;进行视察 |
| 34. shim [ʃim] | | n. 薄垫片 |
| | | vt. 用垫片填 |
| 35. radius ['reidjəs] | | n. 半径(距离) |
| 36. perpendicular [ˌpɜːpən'dikjələ] | | adj. 垂直的,成直角的 |
| 37. intersect [ˌintə'sekt] | | vt. & vi. (指线条、道路等)相交,交叉 |
| 38. protruding [prə'truːdiŋ] | | v. (使某物)伸出,(使某物)突出 |
| 39. spindle ['spind(ə)l] | | n. 轴;纺锤,纱锭 |
| 40. retractable [ri'træktəbl] | | adj. 可收回的;可缩回的;可缩进的 |
| 41. misconception ['miskən'sepʃən] | | n. 误解;错觉;错误想法 |
| 42. squeeze [skwiːz] | | vt. 挤;紧握;勒索 |
| | | vi. 压榨 |
| 43. kinetic [ki'netik; kai-] | | adj. [力]运动的;活跃的 |
| 44. pivot ['pivət] | | n. 枢轴;中心点;旋转运动 |
| 45. caliper ['kælipə] | | n. 卡尺;卡钳制动钳 |
| 46. hub [hʌb] | | n. 轮毂 |
| 47. vent [vent] | | n. 出口;通风孔 |
| | | vt. 放出……;给……开孔 |
| | | vi. 放出 |

## Proper Names

| | |
|---|---|
| 1. the steering linkage | 转向联动装置,转向连杆机构 |
| 2. rack-and-pinion | 齿轮齿条传动装置 |
| 3. recirculating-ball | 循环球式传动装置 |
| 4. steering gear | 转向器 |
| 5. rotary valve | 回转阀 |
| 6. tie rod | 转向横拉杆 |

| | | |
|---|---|---|
| 7. | steering arm | 转向臂 |
| 8. | steering wheel | 转向盘；驾驶盘 |
| 9. | gear reduction | 齿轮减速 |
| 10. | steering ratio | 转向器速比 |
| 11. | pitman arm | 转向摇臂 |
| 12. | ball bearing | 滚珠,钢球；滚珠轴承 |
| 13. | rotary-vane pump | 叶片泵 |
| 14. | rotary Valve | 回转阀 |
| 15. | torsion bar | 扭力杆 |
| 16. | diaphragm spring | 隔膜簧 |
| 17. | drum brake | 鼓式制动器 |
| 18. | disc brake | 盘式制动器 |
| 19. | after a while | 不久,过一会儿 |
| 20. | rear wheel drive | 后轮驱动 |
| 21. | crown gear | 冠齿轮；平面齿轮；差动器侧面伞齿轮 |
| 22. | a set | 一套 |
| 23. | roller bearing | 滚柱轴承 |
| 24. | as opposed to | （表示对比）而,相对于 |
| 25. | the First Law of Thermodynamics | 热力学第一定律 |
| 26. | brake pad | 刹车片；盘式刹车片 |
| 27. | emergency brake mechanism | 紧急制动机构 |
| 28. | self-actuating brake | ［车辆］自动制动 |
| 29. | wedging action | 楔进作用 |

**Notes**

①The clutch connects the two shafts so that they can either be locked together and spin at the same speed, or be decoupled and spin at different speeds.

离合器连接两根轴,这样它既可以使得两者锁在一起同速转动,也可以使两者分开分别以不同的速度转动。

②The friction material on a clutch disc is very similar to the friction material on the pads of a disc brake or the shoes of a drum brake—after a while, it wears away.

离合器盘上的摩擦材料与盘式制动器的夹钳或者鼓式制动器的制动蹄的摩擦材料很相似——使用过程中容易磨损。

③For maximum traction, a four wheel drive machine has been designed with three differentials, separating the front wheels, the rear wheels and the front from the rear, allowing each wheel to turn at its own speed under power.

为得到最大的牵引力,四轮驱动车已设计成装有三套差速器,使前轮之间、后轮之间及后轮与前轮之间彼此分离,容许每个车轮在动力作用下以各自的速度转动。

④A pinion gear, which is splined into the end of the drive shaft, turns a beveled crown gear which is fastened onto the end of one of the axles. An assembly of four small beveled gears (two pinions and two star gears) is bolted to the crown gear and turns with it.

小伞齿轮与主传动轴末端以花键相连接,并带动固定在一后轴轴端的一个冠形大伞齿轮转动。用螺栓连接将4个小伞齿轮(两个小齿轮和两个行星齿轮)与冠形大齿轮装配在一起,并随大伞齿轮转动。

⑤The assembly drives both axles at the same speed when the machine is being driven in a straight line, but allows the axle opposite the crown gear to turn slower or faster, as required.

当传动机构以同速驱动两后轴时,机械便直线行驶。但是,当有需要时,大伞齿轮对面的那一后轴可慢转或快转。

⑥The gear ratio (ratio of the number of teeth on one gear to the number of teeth on the other) between the crown gear and the pinion gear is one of the factors that determine the performance characteristics of the machine, such as acceleration and top speed.

伞齿轮与游星齿轮之间的传动比(一齿轮齿数与另一齿轮齿数之比)是决定机械使用性能,如加速度和最高行速的因素之一。

⑦Today the pinion and crown gears are helical gears, which means that the toothed surfaces are beveled and the teeth themselves are curved. This design eliminates play between the teeth, because as the gears spin together one tooth is in full contact before the previous tooth leaves.

当今的大小伞齿轮都是螺旋齿,即齿轮齿面为锥面,齿轮本身为曲线形。这种设计消除了齿轮间隙,因为在大小齿轮同时旋转时,其任一齿其前一齿离开之前是处于完全接触状态的。

⑧In order to produce a particularly quiet differential, the pinion and crown gears are lapped together in a lapping machine which duplicates the operating conditions of the completed differential.

为生产无噪声的差速器,就要将大、小伞齿轮一起放进研磨机中,按照成品差速器的运转条件进行精研,反复进行研磨。

⑨A rack-and-pinion gear set is enclosed in a metal tube, with each end of the rack protruding from the tube.

整个齿轮齿条式转向器装置金属壳内,其齿条从转向器伸出来与转向摇臂连接。

⑩The balls actually serve two purposes: First, they reduce friction and wear in the gear; second, they reduce slop in the gear.

实际上,这些钢球有两个作用:首先,减少齿轮的摩擦和磨损;其次,可以减少齿轮的松动。

## Exercises

**Choose the best answer from the following choices according to the text.**

A clutch works because of _____ between a clutch plate and a flywheel.

The _____ is a gear assembly in a motor machine which allows the propeller shaft to drive shaft, to turn the machine wheels at different speeds when the machine is going around a curve.

_____ is quickly becoming the most common type of steering on machine.

_____ work on the same principle as disc brakes: Shoes press against a spinning surface.

 A. Rack-and-pinion steering    B. friction    C. differential    D. Drum brakes

# Practical Reading

## Hydraudynamic Transmission

## 液力传动

**Fluid Coupling**

Fluid couplings work on the hydrodynamic principle. It consists of a pump generally known as impeller and a turbine generally known as rotor, both enclosed suitably in a casing. The impeller and rotor is bowl shaped and have large number of radial vanes. ①They face each other with an air gap. The impeller is suitably connected to the prime mover while the rotor has a shaft bolted to it. This shaft is further connected to the driven machine through the suitable arrangement. Oil is filled in the fluid coupling from the filling plug provided on its body. A fusible plug is provided on the fluid coupling which blows off and drains out oil from the coupling in case of sustained overloading. There is no mechanical internal connection between the impeller and the rotor (i. e. driving and driven units) and the power is transmitted by virtue of the fluid filled in the fluid coupling. The impeller when rotated by the prime mover imparts the velocity and energy to the fluid which is converted into mechanical energy in the rotor thus rotating it. The fluid follows a closed circuit of flow from the impeller to rotor through the air gap at the outer periphery and from the rotor to impeller again through the air gap at the inner periphery. To enable the fluid to flow from the impeller to rotor it is essential that there is a difference in "Head" between the two and thus it is essential that there is a difference in speed known as slip, between the two (shown as Figure 4-15).②

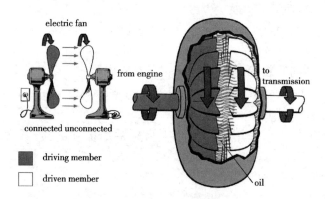

Figure 4-15  Fluid Coupling

Slip is an important and inherent characteristic of a fluid coupling resulting in several desired advantage. As the slip increases, more and more fluid can be transferred from the impeller to the rotor and more torque can be transmitted. However when the rotor is at standstill, maximum fluids is transmitted from the impeller to rotor and maximum torque is transmitted from the coupling. This maximum torque is limiting torque. The fluid coupling also acts a torque limiter.

## Torque Converter

A torque converter is a type of fluid coupling. There are four components inside the very strong housing of the torque converter (shown as Figure 4-16):

- Pump
- Turbine
- Stator
- Fluid

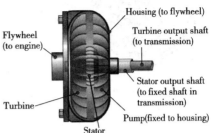

Figure 4-16　Torque-cutaway

The housing of the torque converter is bolted to the flywheel of the engine, so it turns at whatever speed the engine is running at. The fins that make up the pump of the torque converter are attached to the housing, so they also turn at the same speed as the engine.

The pump inside a torque converter is a type of centrifugal pump. As it spins, fluid is flung to the outside. As fluid is flung to the outside, a vacuum is created that draws more fluid in at the center.

The pump section of the torque converter is attached to the housing.

The fluid then enters the blades of the turbine, which is connected to the transmission. The turbine causes the transmission to spin, which basically moves your machine. You can see in Figure 4-17 that the blades of the turbine are curved. This means that the fluid, which enters the turbine from the outside, has to change direction before it exits the center of the turbine. It is this directional change that causes the turbine to spin.

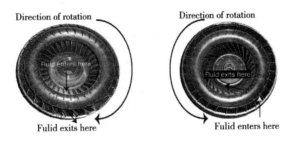

Figure 4-17　Pump-turbine

In order to change the direction of a moving object, you must apply a force to that object. And whatever applies the force that causes the object to turn must also feel that force, but in the opposite direction. So as the turbine causes the fluid to change direction, the fluid causes the turbine to spin.

The fluid exits the turbine at the center, moving in a different direction than when it entered. If you look at the arrows in Figure 4-17, you can see that the fluid exits the turbine moving opposite the direction that the pump or engine is turning. If the fluid were allowed to hit the pump, it would slow the engine down, wasting power. This is why a torque converter has a stator.

### Stator

The stator resides in the very center of the torque converter. Its job is to redirect the fluid returning from the turbine before it hits the pump again. This dramatically increases the efficiency of the

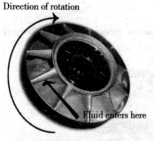

Figure 4-18 Torque-stator

torque converter.

The stator has a very aggressive blade design that almost completely reverses the direction of the fluid. A one-way clutch (inside the stator) connects the stator to a fixed shaft in the transmission (the direction that the clutch allows the stator to spin is noted in Figure 4-18). Because of this arrangement, the stator cannot spin with the fluid—it can spin only in the opposite direction, forcing the fluid to change direction as it hits the stator blades.

## Word List

1. hydrodynamic [haidrəudai'næmik]  *adj.* 水力的；流体动力学的
2. impeller [im'pelə]  *n.* 泵轮
3. turbine ['tə:bain]  *n.* (动力)涡轮
4. fusible ['fju:zəbl]  *adj.* 熔解的，可熔的；易熔
5. impart [im'pɑ:t]  *vt.* 给予(尤指抽象事物)，传授，告知，透露
6. velocity [və'lɔsiti]  *n.* 〈力〉速率；迅速；周转率
7. periphery [pə'rif(ə)ri]  *n.* 外围，边缘；圆周；圆柱体表面
8. standstill ['stæn(d)stil]  *n.* 停顿；停止
9. centrifugal [sentri'fju:g(ə)l]  *adj.* 〈力〉离心的；远中的
   *n.* 离心机；转筒
10. fin [fin]  *n.* 鱼鳍；尾翅；散热片
11. reside [ri'zaid]  *vt.* 住，居住；属于

## Proper Names

1. hydraulic coupling      液力偶合器
2. torque converter        液力变矩器
3. one-way clutch          单向离合器 blows off 放出；吹掉
4. by virtue of            由于，凭借

## Notes

①The impeller and rotor is bowl shaped and have large number of radial vanes.
泵轮和涡轮外形呈碗装，都带有大量径向叶片。

②The fluid follows a closed circuit of flow from the impeller to rotor through the air gap at the outer periphery and from the rotor to impeller again through the air gap at the inner periphery. To enable the fluid to flow from the impeller to rotor, it is essential that there is a difference in "Head" between the two and thus it is essential that there is a difference in speed known as slip, between the two.

油液的流向呈封闭环状，通过外缘的空气隙从泵轮冲向涡轮，再通过内缘的空气隙从涡轮流向泵轮。为保证油液能够从泵轮流向涡轮，两者之间有先后之分是很重要的，因此两轮之间有转速差很重要，被称为滑动。

# 参考答案

**Choose the best answer from the following choices according to the text.**
B C A D

# 项目 5

# 发动机起动系统的介绍

**学习目标**

完成本项目学习任务后,你应当能:
1. 认识关于发动机起动系统的专业术语;
2. 基于所学专业知识,借助专业词典能无障碍地查阅与起动系统相关的英语资料;
3. 正确完成课后练习。

**任务描述**

为什么发动机转速过低时很难实现发动机起动?带着这一问题,完成起动系统相关单词、词汇、特殊语句的学习,掌握起动系统的分类。强化相关专业英文资料的阅读能力。

**引导问题**

引导同学们描述手动起动的过程。

**学　　时**

2 学时

**学习引导**

本学习任务沿着以下脉络进行学习:

复习相关专业知识 → 学习单词和语法 → 通读全文 → 完成课后练习 → 课后阅读

## Project 5　Introduction to the Starting System

Diesel engines are not self-starts. Oppositely, much effort is required to crank a cold engine. It must overcome:

- all of the internal friction caused by the piston rings;
- the compression pressure of any cylinder(s) that happens to be in the compression stroke;

- the energy needed to open and close valves with the camshaft;
- all of the "other" things directly attached to the engine, like the water pump, oil pump, alternator, etc..

Therefore, to start such an engine, it is necessary to spin the crankshaft with sufficient speed for good mixing of air and fuel, adequate compression and ignition of the combustible charge until it receives anther power impulse. The minimum speed with which the crankshaft of an engine should be rotated to ensure reliable starting of the engine is referred to as the cranking speed. It depends on the engine type and starting conditions. The starting speed is 40-50 rpm for carburetor engines and 150-250 rpm for diesel engines. Cranking the engine with a lower speed makes it more difficult for the engine to start, for in this case the charge has more time to escape through leaky joints and give off its heat of compression to the engine components, as a result of which both the pressure and temperature of the charge at the end of the compression stroke are reduced.

It concerns the starting system.

Internal combustion engines may be started by the following methods:

(1) hand starting;

(2) electric starter motor;

(3) gasoline engine;

(4) compressed-air motor and so on.

Of these methods, hand starting depends on the muscle power of the operator to turn the crank handle hooked to the engine crankshaft or to tug at the starting rope wound around the engine flywheel. Generally, it is an auxiliary method in case the storage battery or the starter motor of engines using an electric starting system should fail. And electric motor starting is the most common method used for starting engines.

**Electric Motor Starting**

A typical starting system converts electrical energy into mechanical energy to turn the engine. The starting system consists of the battery, cables, starter motor, solenoid, flywheel ring-gear, the ignition switch and in some cases, a starter relay.

During starting two actions occur:

1) The pinion of the starter motor engages with the flywheel ring gear, and the starter motor then operates to turn over, or 'crank', the engine.

2) The starter motor is an electric motor mounted on the engine block, and operated from the battery. It is designed to have high turning effort at low speeds. When the ignition key is turned to the start position, current flows and energizes the starter's solenoid coil. The energized coil becomes an electromagnet which pulls the plunger into the coil, the plunger closes a set of contacts which allow high current to reach the starter motor. On models where the solenoid is mounted on the starter, the plunger also serves to push the starter pinion to mesh with the teeth on the flywheel. To prevent damage to the starter motor when the engine starts, the pinion gear incorporates an overrunning (one-way) clutch which is splined to the starter armature shaft. The rotation of the running engine may speed the rotation of the pinion but not the starter motor itself. The starting of the engine signals the driver to release the ignition key from the start position, stopping the flow of current to the solenoid

or relay. The plunger is pulled out of contact with the battery-to-starter cables by a coil spring, and the flow of electricity is interrupted to the starter. This weakens the magnetic fields and the starter ceases its rotation. As the solenoid plunger is released, its movement also pulls the starter drive gear from its engagement with the engine flywheel. And in particular, the starter cables are the thickest, as a high current must be delivered to the starter motor, to turn the crankshaft from rest, and keep it turning until the engine fires, and runs on its own (shown as Figure 5-1).

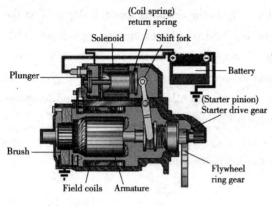

Figure 5-1  Power Stroke

## Battery

The automotive battery, also known as a lead-acid storage battery, is an electrochemical device that produces voltage and delivers current. In an automotive battery we can reverse the electrochemical action, thereby recharging the battery, which will then give us many years of service. The purpose of the battery is to supply current to the starter motor while cranking, to supply additional current when the demand is higher than the alternator can supply and to act as an electrical reservoir.

### Ignition Switch

The ignition switch allows the driver to distribute electrical current to where it is needed.

### Starter Relay

A relay is a device that allows a small amount of electrical current to control a large amount of current. An automobile starter uses a large amount of current (250 + amps) to start an engine. If we were to allow that much current to go through the ignition switch, we would not only need a very large switch, but all the wires would have to be the size of battery cables (not very practical). A starter relay is installed in series between the battery and the starter. Some cars use a starter solenoid to accomplish the same purpose of allowing a small amount of current from the ignition switch to control a high current flow from the battery to the starter. The starter solenoid in some cases also mechanically engages the starter gear with the engine.

### Battery Cables

Battery cables are large diameter, multi-stranded wire which carry the high current (250 + amps) necessary to operate the starter motor. Some have a smaller wire soldered to the terminal which is used to either operate a smaller device or to provide an additional ground. When the smaller cable burns, this indicates a high resistance in the heavy cable. Care must be taken to keep the battery cable ends (terminals) clean and tight. Battery cables can be replaced with ones that are slightly larger but never smaller.

### Starter Motor

The starter motor is a powerful electric motor, with a small gear (pinion) attached to the end. When activated, the gear is meshed with a larger gear (ring), which is attached to the engine. The starter motor then spins the engine over so that the piston can draw in a fuel/air mixture, which is then ignited to start the engine. When the engine starts to spin faster than the starter, a device called an overrunning clutch (bendix drive) automatically disengages the starter gear from the engine gear.

## Word List

1. crank [kræŋk]      n. 曲柄;奇想;〈机〉曲柄轴
        adj. 易怒的
        vt. 装曲柄
2. solenoid ['soulinɔid]      n. 〈电〉螺线管;螺线形电导管
3. battery ['bæt(ə)ri]      n. 〈电〉电池,蓄电池
4. armature ['ɑ:mətjə]      n. 电枢(电动机的部件)
5. diameter [dai'æmitə]      n. 直径
6. ground [graund]      n. 地面;土地
        vt. 使接触地面
7. terminals ['təmənl]      n. 〈计〉终端;终端机;〈电〉接线端子
8. resistance [re'zist(ə)ns]      n. 阻力;电阻;抵抗;反抗;抵抗力

## Proper Names

1. multi-strand      多股的;多线结构
2. piston ring      活塞环
3. ignition switch      点火开关
4. tarter relay      起动继电器
5. battery cable      电池线;蓄电池缆线
6. tarter motor      起动装置;起动电动机
7. bendix drive      惯性式离合器

## Exercises

**Fill in the blanks according to the text.**

Internal combustion engines may be started by the following methods: (1) _____; (2) _____; (3) _____; (4) _____.

# Practical Reading

## The Basic Machine

## 机械基础

Work is performed by applying a force over a distance. These simple machines create a greater output force than the input force; the ratio of these forces is the mechanical advantage of the machine. All six of the simple machines have been used for thousands of years, and the physics behind several of them were quantified by Archimedes (shown as Figure 5-2). These machines can be used together to create even greater mechanical advantage, as in the case of a bicycle.

**Lever**

A lever is a simple machine that consists of a rigid object (often a bar of some kind) and a fulcrum (or pivot). Applying a force to one end of the rigid object causes it to pivot about the fulcrum, causing a magnification of the force at another point along the rigid object. There are three classes of levers, depending on where the input force, output force, and fulcrum are in relation to each other. Baseball bats, seesaws, wheelbarrows, and crowbars are types of levers.

### Wheel & Axle

A wheel is a circular device that is attached to a rigid bar in its center. A force applied to the wheel causes the axle to rotate, which can be used to magnify the force (by, for example, having a rope wind around the axle). Alternately, a force applied to provide rotation on the axle translates into rotation of the wheel. It can be viewed as a type of lever that rotates around a center fulcrum. Ferris wheels, tires, and rolling pins are examples of wheels & axles.

### Inclined Plane

An inclined plane is a plane surface set at an angle to another surface. This results in doing the same amount of work by applying the force over a longer distance. The most basic inclined plane is a ramp; it requires less force to move up a ramp to a higher elevation than to climb to that height vertically. The wedge is often considered a specific type of inclined plane.

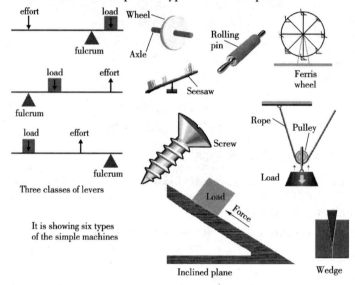

Figure 5-2  The Simple Machines

### Wedge

A wedge is a double-inclined plane (both sides are inclined) that moves to exert a force along the lengths of the sides. The force is perpendicular to the inclined surfaces, so it pushes two objects (or portions of a single object) apart. Axes, knives, and chisels are all wedges. The common "door wedge" uses the force on the surfaces to provide friction, rather than separate things, but it's still fundamentally a wedge.

### Screw

A screw is a shaft that has an inclined groove along its surface. By rotating the screw (applying a torque), the force is applied perpendicular to the groove, thus translating a rotational force into a linear one. It is frequently used to fasten objects together (as the hardware screw & bolt does), although babylonians developed a "screw" that could elevate water from a low-lying body to a higher one (which later came to be known as Archimedes' screw).

**Pulley**

A pulley is a wheel with a groove along its edge, where a rope or cable can be placed. It uses the principle of applying force over a longer distance, and also the tension in the rope or cable, to reduce the magnitude of the necessary force. Complex systems of pulleys can be used to greatly reduce the force that must be applied initially to move an object.

## Word List

| | | |
|---|---|---|
| 1. crank [kræŋk] | n. | 曲柄;奇想;[机]曲柄轴 |
| | vt. | 装曲柄 |
| 2. solenoid [ˈsəʊlənɔɪd] | n. | [电]螺线管;螺线形电导管 |
| 3. battery [ˈbæt(ə)rɪ] | n. | [电]电池,蓄电池 |
| 4. armature [ˈɑːmətʃə; -tʃ(ʊ)ə] | n. | 电枢(电机的部件) |
| 5. diameter [daɪˈæmɪtə] | n. | 直径 |
| 6. ground [graʊnd] | n. | 地面;土地 |
| | vt. | 使接触地面 |
| 7. terminals [ˈtɜːmɪnl] | n. | [计]终端;终端机;[电]接线端子 |
| 8. resistance [rɪˈzɪst(ə)ns] | n. | 阻力;电阻;抵抗;反抗;抵抗力 |

## Proper Names

1. multi-strand — 多股的;多线结构
2. piston ring — 活塞环
3. ignition switch — 点火开关
4. starter relay — 起动继电器
5. battery cable — 电池线;蓄电池缆线
6. starter Motor — 起动装置;起动电动机
7. bendix drive — 惯性式离合器
8. an overrunning (one-way) clutch — 单向/超越离合器
9. flywheel ring-gear — 飞轮齿圈

## 参考答案

**Fill in the blanks according to the text.**

(1) hand starting; (2) electric starter motor; (3) gasoline engine; (4) compressed-air motor

# 项目 6

# 液压系统的介绍

**学习目标**

完成本项目学习任务后,你应当能:
1. 认识关于液压系统的专业术语,熟悉其工作过程及发展状况;
2. 基于所学专业知识,借助专业词典能无障碍地查阅与液压系统相关的英语资料;
3. 正确完成课后练习。

**任务描述**

通过了解液压传动基本原理,完成液压传动相关单词、词汇、特殊语句的学习。强化相关专业英文资料的阅读能力。

**引导问题**

复习液压系统的相关知识要点,分析下图组成及用途。

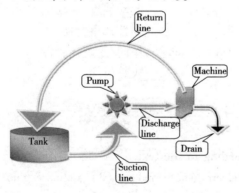

**学　　时**

4 学时

**学习引导**

本学习任务沿着以下脉络进行学习:

# Project 6  Introduction to Hydraulic Systems

The history of hydraulic power is a long one, dating from man's prehistoric efforts to harness the energy in the world around him. The only sources readily available were the water and the wind—two free and moving streams.

**Hydraulic principle**

A Simple hydraulic system consists of two pistons and an oil-filled pipe connecting them (shown as Figure 6-1). The basic idea behind any hydraulic system is very simple: Force that is applied at one point is transmitted to another point using an incompressible fluid according to Pascal's law. The fluid is almost always oil of some sort. The force is almost always multiplied in the process. In this drawing, two pistons (red) fit into two glass cylinders filled with oil (light blue) and connected to one another with an oil-filled pipe. If you apply a downward force to one piston which is the left one in this drawing, then the force is transmitted to the second piston through the oil in the pipe. Since oil is incompressible, the efficiency is very good—almost all of the applied force appears at the second piston. The great thing about hydraulic systems is that the pipe connecting the two cylinders can be any length and shape, allowing it to snake through all sorts of things separating the two pistons. The pipe can also fork, so that one master cylinder can drive more than one slave cylinder if desired.

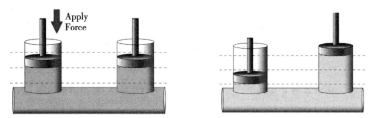

Figure 6-1  A Simple Hydraulic

The neat thing about hydraulic systems is that it is very easy to add force multiplication (or division) to the system. In a hydraulic system, what you can do is to change the size of one piston and cylinder relative to the other, shown as Figure 6-2:

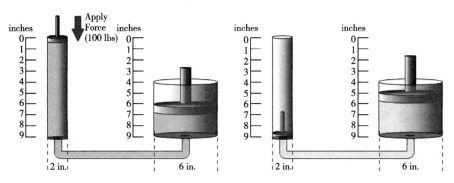

Figure 6-2  Multiplication

To determine the multiplication factor, start by looking at the size of the pistons. Assume that the piston on the left is 2 inches in diameter (1-inch radius), while the piston on the right is 6 inches in diameter (3-inch radius). The area of the two pistons is Pi × $r^2$. The area of the left piston is therefore 3.14, while the area of the piston on the right is 28.26. The piston on the right is 9 times larger than the piston on the left. What that means is that any force applied to the left-hand piston will appear 9 times greater on the right-hand piston. So if you apply a 100-pound downward force to the left piston, a 900-pound upward force will appear on the right. The only catch is that you will have to depress the left piston 9 inches to raise the right piston 1 inch.

The brake in a machine is a good example of a basic piston-driven hydraulic system. When you depress the brake pedal in the machine, it means pushing on the piston in the brake's master cylinder. Four slave pistons, one at each wheel, actuate to press the brake pads against the brake rotor to stop the machine.

### Components

Hydraulic power transmission system are concerned with the generation, modulation, and control of pressure and flow,[①] and in general such systems include (shown as Figure 6-3):

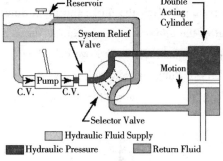

Figure 6-3 The Components of a Hydraulic System

1) Pumps which convert available power from the prime mover to hydraulic power at the actuator.

2) Valves which control the direction of flow, the level of power produced, and the amount of fluid — flow to the actuators. The power level is determined by controlling both the flow and pressure level.

3) Actuators which convert hydraulic power to usable mechanical power. Output at the point required.

4) The medium, which is a liquid, provides rigid transmission and control as well as lubrication of components, sealing in valves, and cooling of the system.

5) Connectors which link the various system components, provide power conductors for the fluid under pressure, and fluid flow return to tank (reservoir).

6) Fluid storage and conditioning equipment which ensure sufficient quality and quantity as well as cooling of the fluid.

### Advantages and disadvantages

The secret of hydraulic system's success and widespread use is its versatility and manageability. Fluid power is not hindered by the geometry operations. And fluid power is the muscle of machine because of advantages in the following four major categories.

1) Ease and accuracy of control. By the use of simple levers and push buttons, the operator of a fluid power system can readily start, stop, speed up or slow down.

2) Multiplication of force. A fluid power system (without using cumbersome gears, and levers) can multiply forces simply and efficiently from a fraction of an ounce to hundreds tons of output.

3) Constant force or torque. Only fluid power systems are capable of providing constant force or torque regardless of speed changes. This is accomplished whether the work output moves from a few

inches per hour to several hundred inches per minute, or from a few revolutions per hour to thousands of revolutions per minute.

4) Simplicity, safety, economy. Generally, fluid power systems use fewer moving parts than comparable mechanical or electrical systems. Thus, they are simpler to maintain and operate. This, in turn, maximizes safety, compactness and reliability.

Additional benefits of fluid power systems include instantly reversible motion, protection against overloads, and infinitely variable speed control. Fluid power systems also have the highest horsepower per weight ratio of any known power source.

The shortcomings of the hydraulic system:

1) As a result of the resistance to fluid flow and leakage, the efficiency is low. If not handled properly, the leakage may not only contamin at sites, but also cause fire and explosion.

2) Vulnerable performance as a result of the impact of temperature change, it would be inappropriate in high or low temperature conditions.

3) The manufacture of precision hydraulic components are expensive.

4) Due to the leakage of liquid medium and the compressibility, the transmission ratio is not accurato.

5) If there is a failure in hydraulic transmission system, it is not easy to find out the reason.

**Large Hydraulic Machines**

One of the best places to get up close and personal with large hydraulic machines is at a construction site. ②The thing that is most amazing about these machines is their sheer size. For example, here is a medium-size shovel/excavator. This machine weighs just over 28 tons, but it can be quite swift in its actions. The bucket can scoop out more than a cubic meter of dirt, which weighs approximately 1 to 1.5 tons, and move it around with no difficulty at all. Moving a person around is trivial (shown as Figure 6-4).

Figure 6-4　Large Hydraulic Machine

## Word List

1. harness [ˈhɑːnis]　　　　　　　　　vt. 利用(自然力)
2. incompressible [ˌinkəmˈpresəbl]　　adj. 不能压缩的
3. multiply [ˈmʌltɪplaɪ]　　　　　　　vt. 乘；使增加；使相乘
　　　　　　　　　　　　　　　　　　vi. 乘；增加
4. snake [sneɪk]　　　　　　　　　　vi. 迂回前进
　　　　　　　　　　　　　　　　　　vt. 拉(木材等)；迂回前进

5. fork [fɔːk]  n. 叉;餐叉;耙
vt. 叉起;使成叉状
vi. 分叉;分歧

6. slave [sleɪv]  n. 从动装置
7. neat [niːt]  adj. 灵巧的;整洁的;优雅的;
8. assume [əˈsjuːm]  vt. 承担;假定;采取;呈现
9. actuator [ˈæktʃʊˌeitə]  n. [自]执行机构;激励者;促动器
10. medium [ˈmiːdɪəm]  n. 媒体;媒介;中间物
11. conductor [kənˈdʌktə]  n. 〈电〉导体;(乐队)指挥;
12. reversible [rɪˈvɜːsɪb(ə)l]  adj. 可逆的;可撤消的;可反转的
13. infinitely [ˈɪnfɪnətli]  adv. 无限地;极其
14. contaminate [kənˈtæmɪneɪt]  vt. 污染,弄脏
n. 受到污染的
15. vulnerable [ˈvʌln(ə)rəb(ə)l]  adj. 易受攻击的,易受…的攻击;易受伤害的
16. impact [ˈɪmpækt]  vt. 影响;撞击;冲突;压紧
vi. 冲击;产生影响
n. 影响;效果;碰撞;冲击力
17. inappropriate [ɪnəˈprəʊprɪət]  adj. 不适当的;不相称的
18. precision [prɪˈsɪʒ(ə)n]  n. 精度,[数]精密度;精确
adj. 精密的,精确的
19. sheer [ʃɪə]  adj. 绝对的
20. excavator [ˈekskəveɪtə]  n. 挖掘机
21. shovel [ˈʃʌv(ə)l]  n. 铁铲
22. bucket [ˈbʌkɪt]  n. 铲斗
23. scoop [skuːp]  vt. 掘;舀取
n. 勺;铲子
24. cubic [ˈkjuːbɪk]  adj. 立方体的,立方的
25. trivial [ˈtrɪvɪəl]  adj. 不重要的,琐碎的;琐细的

## Proper Names

1. dating from  追溯到;始于;起源于
2. hydraulic power  液压动力
3. The only catch is that  唯一的问题是
4. transmission ratio  传动比
5. Pascal's law  帕斯卡定律
6. conditioning equipment  调节设备
7. a fraction of an ounce  每盎司的一小部分
8. regardless of  不顾,不管
9. horsepower per weight ratio  马力/重量比

## Notes

①Hydraulic power transmission system are concerned with the generation, modulation, and control of pressure and flow, and in general such systems include.

液压动力传递系统涉及电动机、调节装置和压力、流量控制。

②One of the best places to get up close and personal with large hydraulic machines is at a construction site.

施工现场是人们能够近距离并以个人的眼光去仔细观察大型液压设备的最佳场所。

## Exercises

**1. Choose the best answer from the following choices according to the text.**

The only sources readily available were _____ and _____ .

_____ which convert available power from the prime mover to hydraulic power at the actuator.

_____ which control the direction of flow, the level of power produced, and the amount of fluid — flow to the actuators.

A. Pumps    B. Valves    C. the wind    D. the water

**2. Translate the following into Chinese.**

1) hydraulic system    2) pump    3) valve    4) tank

# Practical Reading

## Hydraulic Pump Technology
## 液压泵技术

The hydraulic pumps found in virtually all mobile and industrial applications today use pistons, vanes, or gears to create the pumping action that produces flow. Of gear, piston and vane pumps, one type is not better than any other type in an absolute sense—they simply are different, with individual strengths. Each method features individual characteristics that differentiate it from the others and make it suitable for a particular range of applications.

**Piston pumps**

Piston pumps can have the pistons arranged in a radial or axial fashion. Radial types tend to be specialized for applications requiring very high power, while axial piston pumps are available in a wide range of displacements and pressure capabilities that make them suitable for many mobile and industrial tasks.

A xial-piston pumps consist of a set of pistons that are fitted within a cylinder block and driven by an angled swash plate powered by the input shaft. As the swash plate rotates, the pistons reciprocate in their respective cylinder block bores to provide the pumping action (shown as Figure 6-5).

Axial-piston pumps are available with the input shaft and pistons arranged coaxially, or with the input shaft mounted at an angle to the piston bores. Bent axis pumps tend to be slightly more volumetrically efficient for technical reasons, but they also tend to be slightly larger for a given capacity and their shape can present packaging difficulties in some applications.

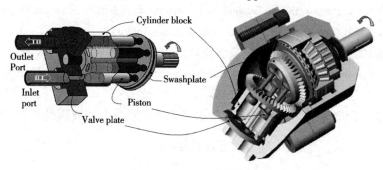

Figure 6-5    Piston Pumps

A unique characteristic of a piston-type pump is that the displacement can be changed simply by changing the angle of the swash plate. Any displacement between zero and maximum is easily achieved with relatively simple actuators to change the swash plate angle.

### Vane pumps

The most commonly encountered vane-type pump generates flow using a set of vanes, which are free to move radially within a slotted rotor that rotates in an elliptical chamber. A typical configuration uses an elliptical cam ring with the rotor spinning within in a cylindrical housing and a pair of side plates to form the pumping chambers[1] (shown as Figure 6-6). The changing volume of the cavity between adjacent vanes creates the pumping action as the rotor rotates.

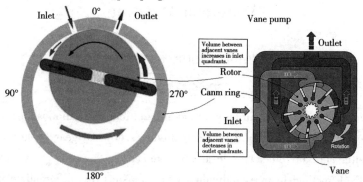

Figure 6-6    Vane Pumps

It is possible to vary the displacement of a vane-type pump (shown as Figure 6-6), but this is not commonly done except for very specialized applications. The majority of the vane-type pumps used in industrial and mobile applications have a fixed displacement.

Vane pumps can be hydraulically balanced, which greatly enhances efficiency. Vane-type pumps are known for being very quiet in operation and producing very little vibration.

### Gear pumps

The simplest gear-type pump uses a pair of mating gears rotating in an oval chamber to produce flow. As the gears rotate, the changing size of the chambers created by the meshing and unmeshing of the teeth provides the pumping action (shown as Figure 6-7).

Another design uses an external rotating ring with internal gear teeth that mesh with an internal gear as it rotates (shown as Figure 6-7). As the inner gear rotates, the tooth engagement creates chambers of diminishing size between the inlet and outlet positions to create flow.

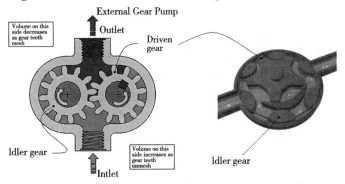

Figure 6-7  Gear Pumps

All gear-type pumps have a fixed displacement. These pumps are relatively inexpensive compared to piston and vane type pumps(with similar displacements), but tend to wear out more quickly and are not generally economically repairable.

**Sweet spots**

Piston-type pumps have a very good service life, provided contamination and heat are controlled. They also have the highest pressure ratings, and the significant advantage of variable displacement. This makes them the best choice for applications where high efficiency and high power density are important considerations. The ability to configure piston-type pumps with both pressure sensing and load sensing capabilities is an important advantage, particularly in mobile applications.

Vane-type pumps are widely used in constant flow/constant pressure industrial applications because they are quiet and easily repaired. They also have the unique attribute of allowing a "soft start".

Gear pumps are very common in constant flow/constant pressure applications on mobile equipment because of their low cost and dirt tolerance. They are also widely used as charge pumps to pressurize the inlets of piston and vane pumps because of their excellent inlet vacuum tolerance.

**Comparing pumps**

Pressure: Piston pumps have the highest pressure capabilities of the three technologies, up to 7250 psi ($500 \times 10^5$ Pa) for those in common use, and as high at 10,000 psi ($690 \times 10^5$ Pa) for certain specialized units. Vane and gear pumps are commonly limited to pressures up to about 4000 psi ($275 \times 10^5$ Pa).

Input Speed: Piston pumps have the highest input speed capabilities.

Power Density: Hydraulic power density is directly related to operating pressure; the higher the pressure the greater the power density. Piston pumps offer the highest power density with vane and gear types following in that order.

Conversion Efficiency: Like power density, the conversion ratio of input power to output power is directly related to operating pressure. Piston pumps offer the highest conversion ratio, followed by vane and gear pumps in that order. The ability of piston and vane pumps to be hydraulically balanced is also a factor in their greater conversion efficiency.

Dirt Tolerance: No hydraulic component is immune to damage from dirt! But of the three pump technologies, the gear-type is the most dirt tolerant, followed by vane and piston pumps in that order.

Inlet Vacuum Tolerance: Positive inlet pressure is always preferred in hydraulic pump applications to avoid wear and premature failure. However, of the three technologies, gear-type pumps are the most vacuum tolerant handling vacuums up to 10 in. -Hg ($254 \times 133$ Pa). Vane-type pumps can handle inlet vacuum up to 6 in. -Hg ($152.4 \times 133$ Pa) and piston-type pumps up to 4 in. -Hg ($101.6 \times 133$ Pa).

Noise and Vibration: Vane-type pumps are the quietest and most vibration-free followed by piston-and gear-type pumps in that order.

Size and Weight: Gear pumps tend to the lightest for a given displacement, followed by vane and piston pumps in that order.

Life Expectancy and Repairability: Piston and vane pumps offer longest service life of the three technologies and both are repairable. Usually only a well-equipped maintenance shop has the capability to repair and test piston pumps. Vane-type pumps are, by far, the easiest to repair. They also have inherent wear compensation built in which helps give them long service life. Gear-type pumps have the shortest service life, and are more often replaced than repaired due to costs.

## Word List

1. feature ['fi:tʃə]  n. 特色,特征;容貌;特写或专题节目
   vi. 起重要作用
   vt. 特写;以…为特色;由…主演
2. specialize ['speʃəlaiz]  vi. 专门从事;详细说明;特化
   vt. 使专门化
3. respective [ri'spektiv]  adj. 分别的,各自的
4. coaxial ['kəu'æksəl]  adj. 同轴的;共轴的
5. displacement [dis'pleism(ə)nt]  n. 取代,移位;排量
6. encounter [in'kauntə]  vt. 遭遇
7. slotted ['slɒtid]  adj. 有沟槽的
8. elliptical [i'liptik(ə)l]  adj. 椭圆的
9. adjacent [ə'dʒeis(ə)nt]  adj. 邻近的,毗连的
10. oval ['əuv(ə)l]  adj. 椭圆的;卵形的
11. sophisticated [sə'fistikeitid]  adj. 复杂的;精致的;久经世故的;富有经验的
    v. 使变得世故;使迷惑
12. variant ['veəriənt]  adj. 不同的;多样的
    n. 变体;转化
13. contamination [kən,tæmi'neiʃn]  n. 污染
14. configure [kən'figə]  vt. 安装;使成形
15. attribute [ə'tribju:t]  n. 属性;特质

## Proper Names

| | |
|---|---|
| 1. be immune to | 对…有免疫力;不受…的影响 |
| 2. premature failure | 过早失效;过早破坏 |
| 3. be available with | 可与 |
| 4. cylinder block | 汽缸体 |
| 5. swash plate | 旋转斜盘 |
| 6. in virtually | 几乎在 |
| 7. bent axis pump | 斜轴式轴向柱塞泵 |
| 8. It is worth noting that | 值得注意的是 |

## Notes

① A typical configuration uses an elliptical cam ring with the rotor spinning within in a cylindrical housing and a pair of side plates to form the pumping chambers.

典型的叶片泵是由定子、转子、泵体和一对侧盘组成泵腔。定子内表面为椭圆形,转子在其内部旋转。

## 参考答案

**1. Choose the best answer from the following choices according to the text.**

C  D  A  B/D  C  A  B

**2. Translate the following into Chinese.**

1)液压系统　　2)泵　　3)阀　　4)油箱

65

# 项目 7

# 筑路机械的介绍

### 学习目标

完成本项目学习任务后,你应当能:
1. 认识关于筑路机械设备的专业术语,熟悉筑路机械设备的施工作业过程;
2. 基于所学专业知识,借助专业词典的帮助能无障碍地查阅与筑路机械设备相关的英语资料;
3. 正确完成课后练习。

### 任务描述

通过本文的学习,完成相关单词、词汇、特殊语句的学习,对筑路机械设备的结构组成、工作过程等方面有一定的认识。强化相关专业英文资料的阅读能力。

### 引导问题

说说你所认识的筑路机械设备有哪些?

### 学　　时

10 学时

### 学习引导

本学习任务沿着以下脉络进行学习:

复习相关专业知识 → 学习单词和语法 → 通读全文 → 完成课后练习 → 课后阅读

## Project 7　Introduction to the Construction Machinery

### Hydraulic Excavator

A hydraulic excavator has three major parts.

Work equipment: this part is for digging and loading.

Upper structure: this part holds components such as a driver's seat, an engine, and so on. Lower structure: this part enables them to move on the ground.

You can see in Figure 7-1.

**Work Equipment**

This is how it works shown in Figure 7-2. This part digs and loads soil. It works just like our arms. Work equipment is run by this hydraulic cylinder. Oil in the cylinder makes the work equipment run. Adjusting the amount of the oil in the cylinder with the control valve, you can move the arm more accurately. And it can transform into several different machines by changing the bucket part.

Figure 7-1  Parts of the Hydraulic Excavator

**Upper Structure**

It is the relation between the engine and oil.

Regular automobiles run with the tires that get power transmitted directly from the engine. However, a hydraulic excavator moves by changing the force from the engine into the hydraulic power.

**Mechanism of Turning**

This part enables a hydraulic excavator to turn around, shown as Figure 7-3. The swing circle of the part makes the upper structure turn. The outer race fixed at the upper structure turns with the pinion that spins along with the inner race fixed at the lower structure. The part between the outer race and the inner race turns smoothly by the ball bearings.

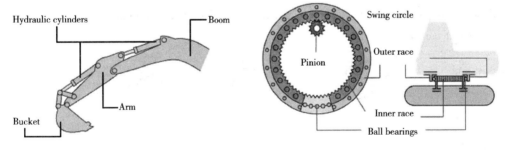

Figure 7-2  Work Equipment                Figure 7-3  Mechanism of Turning

**Lower Structure**

**Different Kinds of Feet**

There are two kinds of feet for hydraulic excavators. Each one has a different characteristic and serves different purposes.

**Wheel Type**

Those ones have tires like regular cars are called "wheel type". They can move to the next construction site running on the road themselves. Since they are not as stable as crawlers, they are not suitable for uneven surfaces, muddy places, or steep hills. They are used more in Europe, because they can move gently without scratching asphalt pavements or old roads made of stones and blocks.

**Crawler Type**

Crawlers can be seen at many construction sites. It literally crawls on the ground. Since more part touches the ground, they do not sink even on the soft surface. Belt-like shaped feet can turn and hold the ground, which enables the machines to go up steep slopes. They can not run on the road like regular cars, so they have to be carried on the big truck when they need to be moved to other locations. This type of feet is very stable.

**The Way of Crawlers' Moving**

Those sheets of iron and rubber are shaped into one big belt. By sending it under the wheels constantly, they can move on any rough roads. Compared to the wheel type, this one has more part touching the ground. It helps them to run on the muddy surface. It is shown in Figure 7-4.

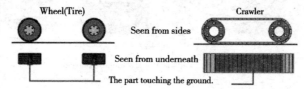

Figure 7-4   Comparing

## Bulldozer

Where did the name come from? Let me explain it for you. Long time ago, people used bulls to cultivate the land. When machines took over their jobs, bulls got time to spare and started dozing. The words, "BULL" and "DOZE" were then combined. That's how a bulldozer got its name. Today, both of "BULLDOZE" and "DOZE" can be used to mean leveling or cultivating the land.

Let's take a look at how each part works in Figure 7-5.

Tractor: It has a driver's seat, an engine, and so forth.

Blade: This part is used to push soil and rocks, and level the ground.

Ripper: It can dig a hard surface.

Figure 7-5   Bulldozer

**Tractor**

Let's look at a driver's seat. You can see in Figure 7-6. The left lever is a tractor motion control joystick. It can make a bulldozer move either back and forth or from side to side. Monitor panel has meters and lamps that tell you the temperature of the water that cools the engine, the temperature of the oil that moves the crawler and the blade, how much fuel is left and so on. The right lever is a blade control joystick. It moves the blade. The brake pedal works just like the one in a regular car. It adjusts speed and stops a bulldozer from moving. Decelerator pedal: Stepping on this pedal, you can reduce the engine rotating. It makes the work easier by changing and adjusting speed of the bulldozer on the smaller degree.

**Blade**

It levels the land in Figure 7-7. A bulldozer can shave the uneven ground, using blade. Then it carries the shaven soil. It also tightens and levels the ground with its own weight.

**Ripper**

It scratches the ground. A larger bulldozer has a nail like part at its back. Ripper can dig big rocks and shave hard ground that blade cannot work on.

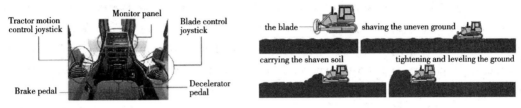

Figure 7-6  A driver's seat          Figure 7-7  The blade

**Classifying**

Bulldozers can be classified as follows:

1) by the mounting of the blade: straight bulldozer, whose blade is perpendicular to the longitudinal axis of the tractor (with the blade in this position the bulldozer pushes to cut earth forward); universal bulldozer, where the blade can be set either perpendicularly to the longitudinal axis of the machine or at an angle (usually 60°) to cast dirt to either side. A universal blade can also be tilted in a vertical plane by an angle of 5° to 8°. A universal blade can push the earth forward and aside, fill up ditches an trenches and shape an earth bed;

2) by the control system: cable bulldozer, whose blade is raised and lowered by a cable hoist driven by a winch mounted on the tractor; hydraulic bulldozer, whose blade is operated by hydraulic cylinders supplied with work fluid by a pump under pressure.

With hydraulic bulldozers, there is a forced penetration of the blade but the smaller speed at which the blade operates makes them inferior to cable bulldozers in shaping work. [1]Hydraulic bulldozers are gaining an ever broader recognition in the world practice;

3) by the type of carrying vehicle: there are crawler and wheel tractors and special air-tyred tractors.

## Road Roller

A road roller is an engineering vehicle of compactor type used to compact soil, gravel, concrete, or asphalt in the construction of roads and foundations, similar rollers are used also at landfills or in agriculture.

The first road rollers were horse-drawn, and were probably just borrowed farm implements (see Figure 7-8). Since the effectiveness of a roller depends on its weight to a large extent, self-powered vehicles replaced horse-drawn rollers from the mid-19th century. The first such vehicles were steam rollers. As internal combustion engine technology improved during the 20th century, kerosene-, diesel-and gasoline-powered rollers gradually replaced their steam-powered counterparts. The first internal-combustion powered road rollers were very similar to the steam rollers they replaced.

Road rollers use the weight of the vehicle to compress the surface being rolled (static) or use mechanical advantage (vibrating). Initial compaction of the substrate on a road project is done by using a pad foot drum roller, which achieves higher compaction density due to the pad' having less surface area. On large freeways, a four wheel compactor with pad foot drum and a blade, such as a Caterpillar 815/825 series machine, would be used due to its high weight, speed and the powerful pushing force to spread bulk material. On regional roads a smaller single pad foot drum machine may be used. The next machine is usually a single smooth drum compactor that compacts the high spots down until the soil is smooth, and this is usually done in combination with a motor grader to get a level surface. Sometimes at this stage a pneumatic tyre roller would be used. These rollers feature two rows (front and back) of pneumatic tyres that overlap. The flexibility of the tyres provides a kneading action that seals the surface and with some vertical movement of the wheels, and enables the roller to operate effectively on uneven ground. Once the soil base is flat the pad drum compactor is no longer used on the road surface. The next course (road base) would be compacted by using a smooth single drum, smooth tandem roller or pneumatic tyre roller in combination with a grader, and a water truck to achieve the desired flat surface with the right moisture content for optimum compaction. Once the road base is compacted, the smooth single drum compactor is no longer used on the road surface (There is however an exception, if the single drum has special flat-wide-base tyres on the machine). The final wear course of asphalt concrete is laid by using a paver and compacted and by using a tandem smooth drum roller, a three-point roller or a pneumatic tyre roller. Three point rollers on asphalt were very common once and are still used, but tandem vibrating rollers are the usual choice now, with the pneumatic tyre roller's kneading action being the last roller to seal off the surface.

Figure 7-8  Horse-drawn road roller

**Variations and Features**

● On some machines, the drums may be filled with water on site to achieve the desired weight. When empty, the lighter machine is easier and cheaper to transport between work sites. On pneumatic tyre rollers the body may be ballasted with water or sand, or for extra compaction wet sand is used. Modern tyre rollers may be filled with steel ballast, which gives a more even balance for better compaction.

● Additional compaction may be achieved by vibrating the roller drums, allowing a small, light machine to perform as well as a much heavier one. Vibration is typically produced by a free-spinning hydrostatic motor inside the drum to whose shaft an eccentric weight has been attached. Some rollers have a second weight that can be rotated relatively to the main weight, to adjust the vibration amplitude and thus the compacting force.

● Water lubrication may be provided to the drum surface from on-board "sprinkler tanks" to prevent hot asphalt sticking to the drum.

● Hydraulic transmission permits greater design flexibility. While early examples used direct mechanical drives, hydraulics reduce the number of moving parts exposed to contamination and allows the drum to be driven, providing extra traction on inclines.

• Human-propelled rollers may only have a single roller drum.

• Self-propelled rollers may have two drums, mounted one in front of the other (format known as "duplex"), or three rolls, or just one, with the back rollers replaced with treaded pneumatic tyres for increased traction.

### Grader

Self-powered graders are used in road construction to excavate side ditches, shape the surfaces and sides of fills and cuts and give them the required gradients.

It can also be utilized for laying earth beds, for leveling and auxiliary jobs, and for building platforms and making profile cuts and banks. In wintertime, self-powered graders are used to clean roads of compacted snow.

A self-powered grader is a highly maneuverable machine, and its blade can be set at various angles both horizontally and vertically or brought out sideways.

The drive comes from the engine to torque converter mounted on the engine, to gear box with transfer box, through a prop shaft to the rear axle, then to the wheels.

The front and rear frames are rigid, welded steel constructions. On the rear frame are mounted engine, gear box, hydraulic and fuel tanks, brake system, driver's cab. On the front, frame are mounted front dozer, blade circle frame and hydraulic cylinders. Front and rear frames are connected by the articulation unit.

The central blade is the main working equipment of a grader. Because of a large range of cutting angles and mould board settings the cutting edge can be set to give the best scrape and cut qualities. The grader blade is attached to the blade circle, this circle is turned by a hydraulic motor via a worm and wheel drive unit. The circle is attached to the circle frame. The circle frame is mounted to the front of the grader frame by means of swivel ball joint. ②Mounted on the back of the grader blade is a ripper. The ripper is used for heavy scarifying work. It is equipped with teeth and operated by a hydraulic cylinder, this cylinder is controlled by a hand operated valve in the main hydraulic valve block.

### Scraper

A scraper removes soil slice by slice, transports and places it in an earthen structure, or pushes it to a dump and then levels it. When moving over freshly dug soil, the scraper partially compacts it. ③

Scrapers are used extensively in road-making, industrial and hydrotechnical construction. It has established an important position in earth moving field. Scrapers can operate on a wide variety of soils, including black earth, sand and clay.

On moist clay and black earth scrapers are not very efficient as the soil sticks to the walls of the bowl and clogs it; they are quite useless on boggy soil as the wheels sink into the mud. Loose sand does not fill the bowl well. Scrapers prove most useful on moderately wet sand soils and loams as they fill the entire volume of bowl. Scrapers must not be used on soils containing large stones. Very heavy soils should be ripped beforehand.

Scrapers can be classified as follows:

(1) By the geometrical capacity of the bowl: 1.5, 3.0, 6.0, 10.0, 15.0, 25.0m³ etc.

(2) By the mode of locomotion: trailer, semi-trailer and self-powered.

(3) By the method of discharge: with free, half-forced and forced discharge.

Free discharge does not empty the bowl completely of sticky and moist soils and is only in low capacity machines. Forced discharge proves most reliable, although it involves a greater consumption of power.

(4) By the system of control: hydraulic or cable control.

The working process of a scraper is as follow: The rear part has a vertically moveable hopper (also known as the bowl) with a sharp horizontal front edge. The hopper can be hydraulically lowered and raised. When the hopper is lowered, the front edge cuts into the soil or clay like a plane and fills the hopper. When the hopper is full it is raised, and closed with a vertical blade (known as the apron). The scraper can transport its load to the fill area where the blade is raised, the back panel of the hopper, is hydraulically pushed forward and the load tumbles out. Then the empty scraper returns to the cut site and repeats the cycle.

## Asphalt Paver

An asphalt paver is a machine used to distribute, shape, and partially compacts a layer of asphalt on the surface of a roadway, parking lot, or other area. It lays the asphalt flat and provides minor compaction before it is rolled by a roller.

It is sometimes called an asphalt-paving machine. Some pavers are towed by the dump truck delivering the asphalt, but most are self-propelled. Self-propelled pavers consist of two major components: the tractor and the screed. The tractor provides the forward motion and distributes the asphalt. The tractor includes the engine, hydraulic drives and controls, drive wheels or tracks, receiving hopper, feeder conveyors, and distribution augers. The screed levels and shapes the layer of asphalt. The screed is towed by the tractor and includes the leveling arms, moldboard, end plates, burners, vibrators, and slope sensors and controls.

## Operation

The asphalt is added from a dump truck or a material transfer unit into the paver's hopper. The conveyor then carries the asphalt from the hopper to the auger. The auger places a stockpile of material in front of the screed. The screed takes the stockpile of material and spreads it over the width of the road and provides initial compaction.

The paver should provide a smooth uniform surface behind the screed. In order to provide a smooth surface a free floating screen is used. It is towed at the end of a long arm which reduces the base topology effect on the final surface. The height of the screen is controlled by a number of factors including : the attack angle of the screed, weight and vibration of the screed, the material head and the towing force.

To conform to the elevation changes for the final grade of the road, modern pavers use automatic screed controls, which generally control the screed's angle of attack from information gathered from a grade sensor. Additional controls are used to correct the slope, crown or superelevation of the finished pavement.

In order to provide a smooth surface the paver should proceed at a constant speed and have a consistent stockpile of material in front of the screed. Increase in material stockpile or paver speed will cause the screed to rise resulting in more asphalt being placed, therefore a thicker mat of asphalt and an uneven final surface. Alternatively a decrease in material or a drop in speed will cause the screed to fall and the mat to be thinner.

The need for constant speed and material supply is one of the reasons for using a material transfer unit in combination with a paver. A material transfer unit allows for constant material feed to the paver without contact, providing a better end surface. When a dump truck is used to fill the hopper of the paver, it can make contacts with the paver or cause it to change speed and affect the screed height.

## Word List

1. excavator ['ekskəveitə]　　　　　n. 挖掘机
2. dig [dig]　　　　　　　　　　　vt. 挖, 掘; 探究
　　　　　　　　　　　　　　　　 vi. 挖掘
3. bucket ['bʌkit]　　　　　　　　n. 桶, 水桶; 铲斗
4. boom [buːm]　　　　　　　　　vt. 使兴旺; 发出隆隆声
　　　　　　　　　　　　　　　　 vi. 急速发展; 发出隆隆声
　　　　　　　　　　　　　　　　 n. 繁荣; 吊杆
5. spin [spin]　　　　　　　　　　vi. 旋转; 纺纱; 吐丝; 晕眩
　　　　　　　　　　　　　　　　 vt. 使旋转; 纺纱; 编造; 结网
　　　　　　　　　　　　　　　　 n. 旋转; 疾驰
6. crawler ['krɔːlə]　　　　　　　 n. 爬行者; 履带牵引装置
7. steep [stiːp]　　　　　　　　　adj. 陡峭的, 不合理的; 夸大的; 急剧升降的
　　　　　　　　　　　　　　　　 vt. 泡; 浸; 使…充满
　　　　　　　　　　　　　　　　 vi. 泡; 沉浸
　　　　　　　　　　　　　　　　 n. 峭壁; 浸渍
8. scratch [skrætʃ]　　　　　　　 n. 擦伤; 抓痕; 刮擦声; 乱写
　　　　　　　　　　　　　　　　 adj. 打草稿用的; 凑合的; 碰巧的
　　　　　　　　　　　　　　　　 vt. 抓; 刮
9. literally ['lit(ə)rəli]　　　　　　adv. 照字面地; 逐字地; 准确的
10. sheet [ʃiːt]　　　　　　　　　n. 薄片, 纸张; 薄板; 床单
　　　　　　　　　　　　　　　　 vt. 覆盖; 盖上被单; 使成大片
　　　　　　　　　　　　　　　　 vi. 成片流动; 大片落下
　　　　　　　　　　　　　　　　 adj. 片状的
11. bulldozer ['buldəuzə]　　　　 n. 推土机
12. cultivate ['kʌltiveit]　　　　　vt. 培养; 陶冶; 耕作
13. spare [speə]　　　　　　　　 vt. 节约, 吝惜; 饶恕; 分出, 分让
　　　　　　　　　　　　　　　　 vi. 饶恕, 宽恕; 节约

*adj.* 多余的;瘦的;少量的
*n.* 剩余;备用零件

14. tractor [ˈtræktə]         *n.* 拖拉机;牵引机
15. blade [bleid]             *n.* 叶片;刀片
16. ripper [ˈripə]            *n.* 撕裂者;粗齿锯;裂具
17. joystick [ˈdʒɔistik]      *n.* 操纵杆,〈机〉控制杆
18. roller [ˈrəulə]           *n.* 〈机〉滚筒;〈机〉滚轴;辊子;滚转机
19. substrate [ˈsʌbstreit]    *n.* 基质;基片;底层
20. bulk [bʌlk]               *n.* 体积,容量;大多数,大部分;大块
                              *vt.* 使扩大,使形成大量;使显得重要
21. regional [ˈriːdʒənl]      *adj.* 地区的;局部的;
22. pneumatic [njuːˈmætik]    *adj.* 气动的;充气的;有气胎的
                              *n.* 气胎
23. row [rəu]                 *n.* 行,排
24. overlap [ˌəuvəˈlæp]       *n.* 重叠;重复
                              *vi.* 部分重叠;部分的同时发生
                              *vt.* 与…重叠;与…同时发生
25. knead [niːd]              *vt.* 糅合,揉捏;按摩;捏制
26. grader [ˈgreidə]          *n.* 平地机
27. scraper [ˈskreipə]        *n.* 〈机〉铲运机
28. paver [ˈpeivə]            *n.* 铺砌工;铺路材料;摊铺机

## Proper Names

1. construction machine              施工机械
2. upper structure                   上部结构
3. work equipment                    工作装置
4. lower structure                   下部结构
5. swing circle                      挖掘机的回转结构
6. outer race                        〈机〉外环
7. monitor panel                     监控板
8. tractor motion control joystick   运动控制操纵杆
9. decelerator pedal                 缓动器踏板
10. pad drum compactor               垫鼓压实机
11. pneumatic tyre roller            轮胎压路机
12. bulldozer                        推土机
13. road roller                      压路机
14. asphalt paver                    沥青摊铺机

## Notes

① …but the smaller speed at which the blade operates makes them inferior to cable bulldozers in shaping work.

……但是刀片操作速度较慢,使得这种推土机在修整施工中不如钢索推土机。

②The circle frame is mounted to the front of the grader frame by means of swivel ball joint.

环形刀架通过滚珠回转支承安装在平地机机架的前部。

③When moving over freshly dug soil, the scraper partially compacts it.

当驶过新挖的土壤时,铲运机对其进行部分压实。

## Exercises

**Translate the following into Chinese.**

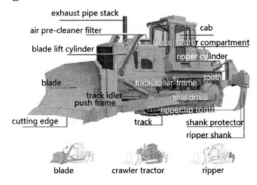

# Practical Reading

## The Asphalt

## 沥青

Paving with asphalt concrete allows you to pave faster, more efficiently, more economically, and with greater serviceability than with any other paving materials in the world. Asphalt Concrete has an absolute advantage in every paving application. Now we will tell you about those advantages.

**Smoothness**

Asphalt will consistently give the driving public the smooth, quiet ride they have come to expect from this product. Asphalt Concrete is machine-placed, so it has a uniform surface unsurpassed by other pavements. Repetitive joints, noisy surface texture, and blowups are eliminated by this method of construction. These features benefit airport users, too. Asphalt Concrete runways and taxiways mean safer landings and takeoffs, because such surfaces are smoother and easier to maintain.

**Staged Construction**

A major advantage for Asphalt Concrete is the potential for staged construction. The asphalt base course can be placed and used under traffic during initial construction. This pavement can then be overlaid with final surface courses. Staged construction improves on-site conditions, removes the aspect of muddy soils, and provides a place to store construction materials and equipment. This method also provides an opportunity to discover and correct unanticipated problem areas, such as a weak subgrade, poor drainage, or poorly compacted trenches, which can be repaired at minimal cost.

### Durability

Asphalt Concrete is a flexible pavement, with same bridging action, which allows it to withstand occasional overloads without serious damage. Its resistance to freeze-thaw and deicing salts allows it to wear better during winter. Its lack of repetitive joints removes the possibility of blowups that plague Portland Cement Concrete during summer. ①Inch for inch, asphalt cement concrete performs better than Portland Cement Concrete.

### Economical

The Federal Highway Administration has shown that a dollar spent on asphalt pavements goes 26.9 percent farther than a dollar spent on concrete pavements. ②That's because asphalt is cost-effective. It has a lower first cost than concrete and it lasts longer. Staged construction helps spread out the cost of placement. Because asphalt pavement has no joints to repair and is not affected by freeze-thaw actions, it is much less expensive to maintain.

### Safety

Asphalt pavements offer high skid resistance values. The dark color of asphalt reduces glare, helps melt ice and snow, and provides a high contrast for lane markings.

### Recyclable

Another major advantage of asphalt concrete is its ability to be completely recycled. Not only can the aggregates be reused, but the asphalt cement binder also retains its cementing properties and can be reused in a new mix. Pavements can be recycled both on site using cold mix or via a hot mix plant. Recycled pavements have been tested and proven in both the laboratory and the field to perform at least as well as virgin aggregate mixes. Over 90 percent of the hot mix asphalt plants in Iowa are capable of using reclaimed asphalt pavement (RAP). ③Asphalt pavements are 100 percent recyclable.

### Versatility

The versatility and popularity of asphalt is evident across the state of Iowa and all America-factories and schools, office parks and playgrounds, and the overwhelming majority of our streets and roads stand as clear testimony that the advantages of asphalt make it America's first choice for paving and rehabilitation.

## Word List

| | | |
|---|---|---|
| 1. asphalt[ˈæsfælt] | n. | 沥青;柏油 |
| | vt. | 以沥青铺 |
| | adj. | 用柏油铺成的 |
| 2. pave[peiv] | vt. | 铺设;安排;作铺设之用 |
| 3. blowup[ˈbləuʌp] | n. | 爆炸;放大;勃然大怒;崩溃 |
| 4. traffic[ˈtræfik] | n. | 交通;运输;贸易;〈通信〉通信量 |
| | vt. | 用…作交换;在…通行 |
| | vi. | 交易,买卖 |
| 5. subgrade[ˈsʌbgreid] | n. | 路基;地基 |
| 6. repetitive[riˈpetitiv] | adj. | 重复的 |
| 7. melt[melt] | vi. | 熔化,溶解;渐混 |

|   |   |   |
|---|---|---|
|   |   | *vt.* 使融化;使熔化;使软化;使感动 |
|   |   | *n.* 熔化 |
| 8. | contrast['kɔntræst] | *vi.* 对比;形成对照 |
|   |   | *vt.* 使对比;使与…对照 |
|   |   | *n.* 对比;差别;对照物 |
| 9. | reclaimed[ri'kleim] | *adj.* 回收的,再生的;翻造的 |
|   |   | *v.* 回收利用 |
| 10. | evident['evid(ə)nt] | *adj.* 明显的;明白的 |
| 11. | overwhelming[ˌovə'welmiŋ] | *adj.* 压倒性的;势不可挡的 |
|   |   | *v.* 压倒;淹没 |
| 12. | testimony['testiməni] | *n.* 〈法〉证词,证言;证据 |
| 13. | rehabilitation['riːhəˌbili'teiʃən] | *n.* 复原 |

## Proper Names

1. staged construction 分期修建;阶段施工
2. freeze-thaw 融化,冻融
3. deicing salts 融雪剂
4. the Federal Highway Administration 联邦高速公路管理局
5. asphalt pavement 沥青混凝土路面
6. concrete pavement 混凝土路面
7. lane marking 车道线
8. RAP 再生沥青混凝土粒料

## Notes

①Its lack of repetitive joints removes the possibility of blowups that plague Portland cement concrete during summer.

沥青混凝土路面与普通水泥混凝土路面不同,不存在重复拼接。夏季期间,沥青路面就不会出现如水泥路面常见的病害(胀缝处剥落及碎裂)。

②The Federal Highway Administration has shown that a dollar spent on asphalt pavements goes 26.9 percent farther than a dollar spent on concrete pavements.

联邦高速公路管理局表示:将同样的1美元用于沥青路面和水泥路面中,沥青路面可以多铺出26.9%的长度。

③Over 90 percent of the hot mix asphalt plants in Iowa are capable of using reclaimed asphalt pavement (RAP).

在爱荷华州,90%以上的沥青拌和设备都可使用再生沥青混凝土粒料进行生产。

## 参考答案

**Translate the following into Chinese.**

exhaust pipe stack 排气烟囱

| | |
|---|---|
| air pre-cleaner filter | 空气预净机过滤器 |
| blade lift cylinder | 铲刀提升油缸 |
| blade | 铲刀 |
| cab | 驾驶室 |
| diesel motor compartment | 柴油发动机室 |
| ripper cylinder | 松土器油缸 |
| tooth | 齿 |
| track roller frame | 履带架 |
| track idler | 履带引导轮 |
| push frame | 推力架 |
| final drive | 最终传动 |
| ripper tip tooth | 松土器的齿 |
| cutting edge | 刀刃 |
| track | 轨道 |
| shank protector | （松土器）柱保护器 |
| ripper shank | 松土器铲柄 |
| blade | 铲刀 |
| crawler tractor | 履带式牵引车 |
| ripper | 松土器 |

# 项目 8

# 路面养护机械的介绍

### 学习目标

完成本项目学习任务后,你应当能:

1. 认识部分路面养护机械、了解其发展状况,掌握路面养护机械的部分专业术语,了解路面养护设备的施工作业以及维护方面注意事项;

2. 基于所学专业知识,借助专业词典的帮助能无障碍地查阅与路面养护机械设备相关的英语资料;

3. 正确完成课后练习。

### 任务描述

通过现代工程机械设备介绍的专业基础铺垫后,完成相关单词、词汇、特殊语句的学习。对路面养护机械设备的结构组成、工作原理、使用维护等方面有一定的认识。强化专业相关英文资料的阅读能力。

### 引导问题

说说你所认识在路面养护机械设备有哪些?

### 学时

6 学时

### 学习引导

本学习任务沿着以下脉络进行学习:

复习相关专业知识 → 学习单词和语法 → 通读全文 → 完成课后练习 → 课后阅读

# Project 8　Introduction to Pavement Maintenance Machinery

## Cold Milling Machines

Milling machines include hot milling machines and cold milling machine (Figure 8-1). Hot milling machines with heating devices are usually used on operation of hot recycling roads.

The cold milling machines are used to remove the defective paving to the required thickness so that it can be replaced and the carriageway can be repaired. The reclaimed asphalt pavement can be reused in stationary mixing plants without requiring further treatment.

Cold milling machines are also used to remove strips of asphalt pavement so that supply lines can be installed in trenches, thus ensuring that the time required for the road works is kept short.

The complete product range currently encompasses 16 types of milling machinery and is designed to meet all the various requirements for processing pavement, from partial repair of areas to complete removal of entire road structures.

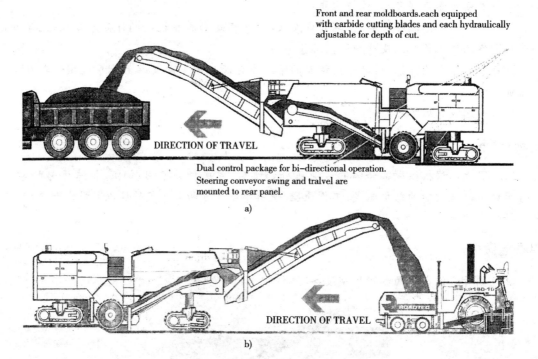

Figure 8-1　Cold Milling Machine
a) Front Loading Up Cutting; b) Rear Loading Down Cutting

The complete product range currently encompasses 16 types of milling machinery and is designed to meet all the various requirements for processing pavement, from partial repair of areas to complete removal of entire road structures.

The cold milling machines consist of power unit, chassis, milling drum assembly, milling depth control (Automatic leveling system), hydraulic system, electric system, loading milled material system and other auxiliary equipments.

The milling machines can be classified as front loading up cutting and rear loading down cutting types.

The (W2100) milling machine is crawler-typed and mechanically driven milling drum and a two-stage front loading conveyor system, which can be adjusted in height and slewed to both sides. The crawler track is suspended on the chassis by means of cylindrical with hydraulic height adjustment. The height of each crawler track can be adjusted individually. The milling depth is set via the two front columns, while the rear crawler tracks act as a full floating axle. The large stroke provides a large ground clearance, thus facilitating even difficult maneuvers, such as revering in the milled track or loading the machine onto a low-bed trailer. The machine can be securely lashed onto a lowbed trailer or loaded by crane with the aid of lashing lugs. A powerful horn and the comprehensive working and safety lights, together with a freely position able lamp with magnetic pedestal, provide sufficient illumination, thus ensuring that the machine can be operated safely, even in inclement weather.

The milling drum operates in up-milling direction. Tool holders accommodating the point-attack cutting tools are welded onto the drum body. Special edge segments ensure a clean sharp cut at the edges. Additional ejectors ensure that the milled material is efficiently transferred to the primary conveyor. If the milled material is to remain on the ground, a flap at the scraper blade ensures that it is deposited between the crawler tracks. As an, option, the milling drum can be equipped with patented and established quick change tool holder system. With this system, the bottom parts of tool holders are welded onto the drum body. The upper parts are secured to the bottom parts by retaining bolts to allow quick replacement. The milling drum is driven mechanically by the diesel engine via a mechanical clutch and power belts acting on the drum gearbox. The power belts ensure optimum power transmission due to their width and the use of 12 V-belt, and have a long service life. Constant tension of the power belts is automatically maintained by a hydraulic cylinder.

The scraper blade opens hydraulically (can be slewed by 100°), thus providing good access to the milling drum for replacement of cutting tools.[①] Sufficient depositing space for the cutting tool containers is provided at both rear crawler tracks.

Loading of the milled material from the milling chamber on trucks is affected to the front (front loading) by means of a wide conveyor system consisting of a primary conveyor and a discharge conveyor.

A gradation control beam largely prevents the asphalt from breaking into slabs and simultaneously protects the primary conveyor against premature wear and tear. The discharge conveyor can load trucks from a great height, its height is adjustable and can be slewed to both sides, thus always allowing an optimum adaptation to the conditions prevailing on site.[②]

The high conveying speed and the generously dimensioned, wide, V-ribbed steep-incline belts ensure that the material is quickly removed from the drum housing.

The discharge conveyor is covered to prevent clouds of dust from being blown away by the wind and causing a nuisance. The design of the conveyor system allows an easy replacement of the belts.

The milling machine is equipped with an electronic automatic leveling system to control the milling depth. It is governed by means of proportional control, meaning that changes in the height of the reference plane are compensated quickly and without overshooting of the machine.

The reference planes can be scanned by various methods, for instance, by a wire-rope sensor at the side plates, an ultrasonic sensor on the existing road surface, a grade-line in combination with rotary transducers, or a plane formed by lasers. ③A slope control sensor is available as an equipment option; the required connections are included as a standard feature.

The multiplex system can also be integrated into the automatic leveling system as an equipment option. It is an equalizing system for longitudinal leveling.

A hydraulically operated water supply system cools the point-attack cutting tools during milling, thus considerably extending their service life. The water pressure and quantity can be adjusted from operator's platform. The spray nozzles are easily removed for cleaning.

In addition, both the primary and the discharge conveyor can be sprinkled separately at several points. The continuous sprinkling of the drum and the conveyor system effectively prevents the development of dust.

An automatic hose reel is additionally mounted at the front of the chassis as a standard feature to enable cleaning of the machine. The desired water quantity and the water pressure can be adjusted from the ground. Water is filled via a C-pipe connection or a large filling port.

## Hot Recycling Machines

The hot recycling method is used to repair bituminous bound surface courses by replastifying the pavement and admixing binders and additional mixing material.

This method permits on-site restoration of the service properties of the pavement while making complete reuse of the existing road materials. ④

The addition of bind and virgin asphalt material is precisely metered so that the quality of the surface course to be rehabilitated can be improved.

Hot recycling machine is illustrated in Figure 8-2 for rehabilitating large areas of bituminous bound carriageways. Infinitely variable working width for taking up and placing the material is mixed with binder and virgin asphalt. It can operate continuously to on-site heat, scarify, mix, pave and compact. It includes recycling heater, recycling machine, feeding device of admixture, scarify, mixer, remixture paving device, feeding device of additive material, screed and grade and slope control of screed.

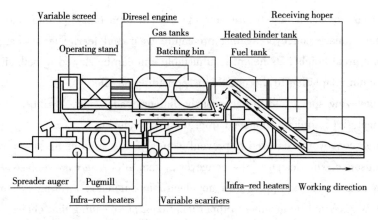

Figure 8-2   Hot Recycling Machine Parts

Self-propelled compact unit is used for rehabilitating bituminous pavement (wearing course and binder course). Rehabilitating is done either by profiling the existing pavement and covering it with a new layer (repaying), or by mixing in an additive and relaying the mix (remixing).

The existing pavement is softened by infrared heaters. The base material is also heated in this way before the mixture is laid (hot-in-hot placing). The energy source used is propane gas, which is vaporized and burnt in gaseous form.

Gas tanks: Double tank for liquid gas, with level indicator.

Vaporizer: Two gas-operated vaporizers with thermostatic control.

Heating elements: All-metal heaters, can be swung out individually to suit the working width.

Heating capacity: Control valves for distributing the heat output in the individual heaters (setting the working pressure).

The admixture specified by laboratory is loaded into the remixer in batches from trucks and is continuously mixed into the reclaimed material in the appropriate proportions.

Receiving hopper: Capacity approx. $3m^3$ with hydraulically tilting side walls. Pushing rollers to push the truck during the unloading process.

Inclined conveyor: Robust scraper conveyor with wear-resisting drag slats and roller chains, hydrostatically driven. The conveyor tunnel is heated so that the mix does not cool down.

Batch bin: Supply container for the admixture with push in metering devices. Measuring is infinitely adjustable.

Chassis conveyor: Robust scraper conveyor with wear-resisting drag slats and roller chains, hydrostatically driven and infinitely adjustable. The conveyor tunnel is heated. The admixture is either fed into the mixer (flap opened hydraulically) or in front of the screed.

Automatic quantity control: The pre-selected quantity to be added (per $m^2$) is continuously monitored by controlling the chassis conveyor in accordance with the forward advance speed of the machine.

The softened pavement is loosened by the rotating scarifier shafts with cutter teeth and augered into the machine with the help of the leveling blades. The working width can be infinitely adjusted via the hydraulic system.

The scarifier unit: The unit consist of two scarifier shafts and leveling bladers which auger the material inwards and two shafts with leveling blades for augering the material to the mixer. [5]

Suspension: The scarifier unit is suspended on rods positioned on both sides and is positioned by two hydraulic cylinders in accordance with the desired loosing depth.

Loosing depth: An automatic device keeps the selected loosening depth constant.

A compulsory pugmill mixer thoroughly mixes the reclaimed material with the admixture until it forms a homogeneous mass.

Mixer: Horizontal twin-shaft compulsory pugmill mix with high-strength lining, hydrostatically driven. The mixer is heated.

The prepared material is discharged from the mixer in a window and accurately placed to profile by the infinitely variable screed. [6]

Compacting screed: Hydraulically adjustable, working width 3m to 4m. Hydraulically operated tampering and vibrating screed for high precompaction. Surface profile can be adjustment.

Bitumen tank: Capacity approx. 1500 litres. It can be fed with liquid bitumen or with bitumen blocks. It is equipped with a thermostatically controlled heating oil heater.

Bitumen pump: Quantity to be added can be infinitely adjusted via the pump speed.

Metering control: The preselected quantity to be added (per m$^2$) is continuously monitored by an automatic control device by controlling the binder pump in accordance with the forward speed of the machine.

Spraying device: Heated spraying tube with nozzles. The bitumen is sprayed in front of the two shaft pugmill mixer and thoroughly mixed in the mixer.

Grade and slope control for screed consist of two grade control and one slope control. The reference levels are sensed either on the side plates or on taut wires.

Hydrostatically driven brushes for cleaning the joints adjacent to the existing pavement located in front of the screed.

An additional screed for precise paving of the existing asphalt pavement which has been sprayed with bitumen prior to overly.

## Word List

1. carriageway ['kæridʒwei]　　　　　n. 车道;马路
2. reclaim [ri'kleim]　　　　　　　　vt. 要求归还、开垦
3. manoeuvre [mə'nu:və]　　　　　vt. 调度,超重
4. slew [slu:]　　　　　　　　　　　vi. 扭转;侧滑;转向;猛拐
5. patent [peit(ə)nt]　　　　　　　vt. 取得专利权
　　　　　　　　　　　　　　　　　　n. 专利权;执照;专利品
6. established [ə'stæbliʃt]　　　　　adj. 得到承认的
7. lash [læʃ]　　　　　　　　　　　vt. 临时安装;扎捆
8. nuisance ['nju:s(ə)ns]　　　　　n. 讨厌的人;状况;麻烦事
9. reel [ri:l]　　　　　　　　　　　vi. 卷;缠;绕
　　　　　　　　　　　　　　　　　　n. 电缆盘,绕线盘
10. inclement [in'klem(ə)nt]　　　　adj. 险恶的;严酷的
11. multiplex ['mʌltipleks]　　　　　adj. 多元的;多路传输的
12. prevail [pri'veil]　　　　　　　vi. 盛行,流行;胜过
13. dimension [di'menʃən]　　　　　n. 尺寸;复面积,体积
14. sprinkle ['spriŋk(ə)l]　　　　　vt. 洒;淋
15. illumination [i,lju:mi'neiʃən]　　n. 照明;〈光〉照度
16. lug [lʌg]　　　　　　　　　　　n. 支托;凸缘;耳状物
　　　　　　　　　　　　　　　　　　vi. 拉,拖
17. premature ['premətjuə]　　　　adj. 早产的;不成熟的
18. replastify [ri'plæstifai]　　　　vt. 再塑,重塑
19. pugmill [pʌgmil]　　　　　　　n. 拌泥机
20. restoration [restə'reiʃ(ə)n]　　n. 恢复;复位;归还

21. virgin ['və:dʒin]  *adj.* 原本的;纯洁的;首创的
22. vaporizer ['veipəraizə]  *n.* 汽化器;喷雾器;蒸馏器
23. scarifier ['skærifaiə]  *n.* 划痕器;松土机
24. rehabilitate [ri:hə'biliteit]  *vt.* 恢复,修复,更新
25. propane ['proupein]  *n.* 丙烷
26. pendulum ['pendjuləm]  *n.* 钟摆;摇锤
27. compulsory [kəm'pʌls(ə)ri]  *adj.* 义务的;被迫的;被强制的
28. taut [tɔ:t]  *adj.* 拉紧的;紧张的

## Proper Names

1. asphalt pavement — 沥青混凝土路面
2. low-bed trailer — 低车架拖车
3. retaining bolt — 固定螺栓
4. up-milling direction — (刀具)从下向上铣削
5. milling drum — 铣刨鼓
6. C-pipe connection — C 型管接头
7. filling port — 加水口
8. V-ribbed steep-incline belt — 带螺纹的提升三角皮带
9. discharge conveyor — 卸料输送器
10. true to — 符合,保证
11. inclined conveyor — 斜置传送带
12. loosening depth — 铣刨深度
13. bitumen spray system — 沥青喷射系统
14. grade and slope control — 坡度控制
15. vibrating screed — 振动式与熨平板

## Notes

①The scraper blade opens hydraulically (can be slewed by 100°), thus providing good access to the milling drum for replacement of cutting tools.

刮板由液压装置开启(能被转动 100°),为更换铣刨滚筒上的切削刀具提供了良好的通道。

②The discharge conveyor can load trucks from a great height, its height is adjustable and can be slewed to both sides, thus always allowing an optimum adaptation to the conditions prevailing on site.

卸料输送器可以从很高的位置给载货车卸料,卸料的高度是可调的且可向两边转动,因此,总是能最佳的适应工地条件。

③The reference planes can be scanned by various methods, for instance, by a wire-rope sensor at the side plates, an ultrasonic sensor on the existing road surface, a grade line in combination with rotary transducers, or a plane formed by lasers.

参考平面可以用不同的方法进行扫描,比如,可以用侧板上的钢丝绳传感器,对现有的路

面使用超声波传感器,对道路纵剖面使用旋转式传感器或用激光形成的表面作为参考。

④This method permits on-site restoration of the service properties of the pavement while making complete reuse of the existing road materials.

这种方法可以在现场恢复道路的使用性能,而且可以重新使用全部现有的道路材料。

⑤The unit consist of two scarifier shafts and leveling blades which auger the material inwards and two shaft with leveling blade for augering the material to the mixer.

翻松装置包括两个转子和(按螺旋线布置的)刀头,刀头将翻松的材料向内聚集,且将材料输送到搅拌器内。

⑥The prepared material is discharged from the mixer in a window and accurately placed to profile by the infinitely variable screed.

备好的混合料从搅拌器的卸料口卸出,并由无级变宽的熨平板精确的摊铺形成路面轮廓。

## Exercises

**1. Put the following expressions into Chinese.**

(1) Hot milling machines with heating devices are usually used on operation of hot recycling road.

(2) The cold milling machines are used to remove the defective paving to the required thickness.

(3) The milling machines can be classified as front loading up cutting and rear loading down cutting types.

(4) The milling machine is equipped with an electronic automatic leveling system to control the milling depth.

(5) The water pressure and quantity can be adjusted from operator's platform.

**2. Fill in the blanks with proper words.**

(1) A slope control sensor is _____ as an equipment option; the required connections are included as a standard feature.

(2) The continuous sprinkling of the drum and the _____ effectively prevents the development of dust.

# Practical Reading

## Asphalt Pavement Maintenance
## 沥青路面的养护

**Clean and Seal**

Clean and seal, used on all types of cracks, involves blowing out crack debris using a hot-air lance or compressed air and then filling with a sealant.

Perform when temperatures are moderately cool, as in spring and fall.

Reroute traffic until the sealant material cures. If the roadway must be opened immediately after sealing, protect the sealant against pick-up by tires by lightly covering the sealant material with fine sand or toilet paper.

Note that moisture will prevent bonding of the crack sealer to the crack walls.

Operation steps:

1. Dry thoroughly with hot-air lance or high-pressure air hose(shown as Figure 8-3).
2. Fill dean crack with sealant(shown as Figure 8-4).
3. Strike off sealant with squeegee to create over-band(shown as Figure 8-5).

  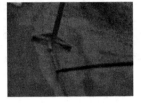

Figure 8-3  Drying        Figure 8-4  Filling Dean Crack        Figure 8-5  Striking off Sealant

### Rout and Seal

Rout and seal, used on transverse and longitudinal cracks, involves using a pavement saw or router to create a reservoir centered over existing cracks, and then filling with a sealant.

Standard specification calls for a 3/4-inch by 3/4-inch reservoir(shown as Figure8-6), but you may adjust the size depending on the sealant. Level the sealant with a 3/4-inch over-band. Make a second pass with additional filler.

Placing an over-band is acceptable; however, consider motor-cycle traffic. When longitudinal cracks are sealed, especially on curves, tires may slip when traveling over the over-band material. This can be very dangerous and should be avoided when sealing longitudinal cracks on curves.

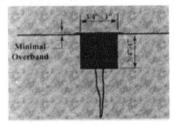

Figure 8-6  3/4-inch × 3/4-inch Reservoir

Apply when temperatures are moderately cool, as in spring and fall.

Reroute traffic until the sealant material cures. If the roadway must be opened immediately after sealing, protect the sealant against pick-up by tires by lightly covering the sealant material with fine sand or toilet paper.

### Full-Depth Crack Repair

Full-depth crack repair involves milting a trench centered over an existing crack, placing hot-mix asphalt into the reservoir in one or more lifts, and compacting to achieve density.

Milling depth varies from 1/2 inch for cracks in good condition to full depth for pavements with severe deterioration in the crack vicinity. The mill width varies from 10 to 12 inches for shallow milling to 3 to 4 inches for deep milling. When choosing the configuration of the area to be milled, the trench should be wide enough to ensure good compaction. It Is difficult to achieve good compaction in a deep and narrow trench.

Release traffic after mixture has been compacted and cured.

Properly drain cracks that have been milled and cleaned out if they are allowed to stand before new asphalt course is placed.

Workmanship and density is very important.

Figure 8-7  Mill and Sweep Crack to Remove any Lose Material

Sequence:
1) Mill out the crack.
2) If needed, use a skid loader to remove millings from the roadway(shown as Figure 8-7).
3) Vacuum out the reservoir.
4) Tack the reservoir with asphalt emulsion.
5) Place hot mix into the reservoir in lifts <4 inches (shown as Figure 8-8).
6) Compact the reservoir with roller so that patch is flush with adjacent pavement(shown as Figure 8-9).

Figure 8-8  Place Hot Mix Neatly in Reservoir

Figure 8-9  Compact the Hot Mix

**Spray Injection Patching**

Spray injection patching, also referred to as blow patching, uses air pressure to apply asphalt emulsion and aggregate into large cracks and potholes.

- Minimize oil use.
- A skilled operator is required for a quality patch.
- Allow traffic over the repaired areas as soon as maintenance workers and equipment are clear.

The spray-injection procedure consists of the following steps:
1) Blow water and debris from the pothole.
2) Spray a tack coat on the sides and bottom of the pothole.
3) Blow asphalt and aggregate into the pothole.
4) Cover the patched area with a layer of aggregate.

## Word List

1. cracks[kræk]　　　　　　　　　n. 裂缝,裂纹;龟裂;板间间隙
2. moderately['mɑdərətli]　　　　adv. 适度地;中庸地;有节制地
3. sealant['siːlənt]　　　　　　　n.〈机〉密封剂
4. moisture['mɔistʃə]　　　　　　n. 水分;湿度;潮湿;降雨量
5. squeegee['skwiːdʒiː]　　　　　n. 橡胶滚轴;橡胶扫帚,橡胶清洁器
　　　　　　　　　　　　　　　　vt. 用橡胶滚轴压;使用橡胶扫帚
6. reservoir['rezəvwɑː(r)]　　　　n. 水库;蓄水池

7. specification [ˌspesifiˈkeiʃ(ə)n]　　　　　n. 规格；说明书；详述
8. longitudinal [ˌlɔn(d)ʒiˈtjuːdin(ə)l]　　　adj. 长度的，纵向的；经线的
9. curves [kəv]　　　　　　　　　　　n. 曲线；弯曲状
10. density [ˈdensiti]　　　　　　　　　n. 密度
11. configuration [kənˌfigəˈreiʃ(ə)n;]　　　n. 配置；结构；外形
12. workmanship [ˈwɔːkmənʃip]　　　　n. 手艺，工艺；技巧
13. sequence [ˈsiːkw(ə)ns]　　　　　　n.〈数〉〈计〉序列；顺序；续发事件
　　　　　　　　　　　　　　　　　　vt. 按顺序排好
14. vacuum [ˈvækjuəm]　　　　　　　n. 真空；空间；真空吸尘器
　　　　　　　　　　　　　　　　　　adj. 真空的；利用真空的；产生真空的
　　　　　　　　　　　　　　　　　　vt. 用真空吸尘器清扫
15. emulsion [iˈmʌlʃ(ə)n]　　　　　　　n.〈药〉乳剂；〈物化〉乳状液；感光乳剂

## Proper Names

1. hot-air lance　　　　　　　　　　热风枪
2. high-pressure air hose　　　　　　高压空气软管
3. strike off　　　　　　　　　　　　砍掉；勾销；击断；印刷
4. pavement saw　　　　　　　　　铺面锯机
5. centered over　　　　　　　　　　集中在
6. motorcycle traffic　　　　　　　　机动车
7. fine sand　　　　　　　　　　　　细砂
8. toilet paper　　　　　　　　　　　卫生纸，厕纸
9. pick-up　　　　　　　　　　　　提取；搭便车
10. full depth　　　　　　　　　　　大切削深度；大吃刀
11. cleaned out　　　　　　　　　　清除，打扫干净
12. skid loader　　　　　　　　　　滑移装载机
13. flush with　　　　　　　　　　　齐平的
14. referred to　　　　　　　　　　被提及；被交付
15. aggregate into　　　　　　　　　聚合成

# 参考答案

**1. Put the following expression into Chinese.**
(1) 带有加热装置的热再生设备常用于道路的热再生施工中。
(2) 冷铣刨机是用于按照所需的厚度来削除缺陷铺层的。
(3) 铣刨机有前方卸料和后方卸料两种工作方式。
(4) 铣刨机配备了一个电子自动调平系统来控制铣削深度。
(5) 水的压力和数量可以在操作面板上进行调整。

**2. Fill in the blanks with proper words.**
(1) available　　　(2) conveyor system

# 项目 9
# 设备维护的介绍

**学习目标**

完成本项目学习任务后,你应当能:

1. 了解常见设备的常见维护方法与内容;掌握设备维护方面的部分专业术语,了解设备维护作业方面的注意事项;
2. 基于所学专业知识,借助专业词典能无障碍地查阅与机械设备维护方面的英语资料。

**任务描述**

以卡特皮勒挖掘机的简单维护为例,完成相关单词、词汇、特殊语句的学习。对工程机械设备的维护、修理等方面有一定的认识。强化专业相关英文资料的阅读能力。

**引导问题**

说说你所知道的工程机械常见的维护作业内容有哪些,如何操作?

**学　　时**

2 学时

**学习引导**

本学习任务沿着以下脉络进行学习:

# Project 9　Introduction to the Maintenance of Construction Machinery

## Battery or Battery Cable-Inspect/Replace
### Warning

Personal injury can result from battery fumes or explosion batteries giving off flammable fumes that can explode. Electrolyte is an acid and can cause personal injury if it contacts the skin or eyes.①

Prevent sparks near the batteries. Sparks could cause vapors to explode. Do not allow jumper cable ends to contact each other or the engine. Improper jumper cable connections can cause an explosion.

Always wear protective glasses when working with batteries.

Operation steps:

1) Turn the engine start switch key to the OFF position. Turn all of the switches to the OFF position.

2) Turn the battery disconnect switch to the OFF position. Remove the key.

3) Disconnect the negative battery cable at the Battery.

4) Disconnect the positive battery cable at the Battery.

5) Disconnect the battery cables at the battery disconnect switch. The battery disconnect switch is connected to the machine frame.

6) Make necessary repairs or replace the battery.

7) Connect the battery cable at the battery disconnect switch.

8) Connect the positive battery cable of the battery.

9) Connect the negative battery cable of the battery.

10) Install the key and turn the battery disconnect switch to the ON position.

## Cooling System Coolant Extender(ELC)-Add
### Warning

Personal injury can result from hot coolant, steam and alkali.

At operating temperature, engine coolant is hot and under pressure. The radiator and all lines to heaters or the engine contain hot coolant or steam. Any contact can cause severe burns.②

Remove cooling system pressure cap slowly to relieve pressure only when engine is stopped and coaling system pressure cap is cool enough to touch with your bare hand.

Do not attempt to tighten hose connections when the coolant is hot, the hose can come off causing bums.

Cooling System Coolant Additive contains alkali avoiding contact with skin and eyes.

### Notice

Mixing ELC with other products will reduce the effectiveness of the coolant.

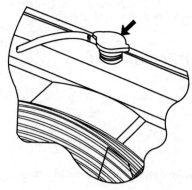

1) Park the machine on level ground.
2) Stop the engine.
3) Unlatch the engine hood and raise the engine hood.
4) Make sure that the cooling system has cooled down. Loosen the cooling system pressure cap slowly in order to relieve system pressure (shown as Figure 9-1).

Note: Refer to Operation and Maintenance Manual "General Hazard Information" for information on containing fluid spillage.

Figure 9-1  Loose Pressure Cap

5) It may be necessary to drain some coolant from the radiator so that Caterpillar Extender can be added to the cooling system.

Note: Always discard drained fluids according to local regulations.

6) Add Caterpillar Extended Life Coolant (ELC) to the cooling system. Refer to the following topics for the proper amount of Caterpillar Extender.

7) Inspect the gasket of the cooling system pressure cap. If the gasket is damaged, replace the pressure cap.

8) Install the cooling system pressure cap.

9) Close the engine hood and latch the engine hood.

## Word List

1. injury['indʒəri]　　　　　　n. 伤害,损害
2. fumes[fjumz]　　　　　　　n. 烟气;激动
3. flammable['flæməbl]　　　　adj. 易燃的;可燃的;可燃性的
4. electrolyte[i'lektrəlait]　　　n. 电解液,电解质;电解
5. acid['æsid]　　　　　　　　n. 酸;迷幻药 adj. 酸的;讽刺的;刻薄的
6. sparks[spɑrks]　　　　　　n. 火花
7. negative['negətiv]　　　　　adj. [数]负的;消极的;否定的;阴性的
　　　　　　　　　　　　　　n. 否定;负数;[摄]底片
　　　　　　　　　　　　　　vt. 否定;拒绝
8. cable['keib(ə)l]　　　　　　n. 电缆
9. coolant['kuːl(ə)nt]　　　　　n. 冷却剂
10. alkali['ælkəlai]　　　　　　n. 碱;可溶性无机盐 adj. 碱性的
11. unlatch[ʌn'lætʃ]　　　　　vt. 拉开(门等的)插栓

## Proper Names

1. result from　　　　　　　　起因于;由……造成
2. attempt to　　　　　　　　 试图,尝试

## Notes

①Electrolyte is an acid and can cause personal injury if it contacts the skin or eyes.

电解液是一种酸性物质,如果让电解液接触皮肤或者眼睛的话会造成伤害。

②At operating temperature, engine coolant is hot and under pressure. The radiator and all lines to heaters or the engine contain hot coolant or steam. Any contact can cause severe burns.

在正常的工作温度范围内,发动机冷却液是很热并且带压力。散热器和所有与其连接的管道(管道连接发热器或发动机)都有热的冷却剂或蒸汽,接触到他们都可以造成严重灼伤。

## Exercises

**Read the following content and translate into Chinese:**

**Belt-Inspect/Adjust/Replace**

Note: This engine is equipped with a belt tightener that automatically adjusts the belt to the correct tension.

1) Unlatch the engine hood and raise the engine hood.

2) Inspect the belt for wearing and for cracking.

3) If the belt requires replacement, perform the following steps:

a. Remove the upper fan guard (shown as Figure 9-2).

b. Rotate the belt tensioner clockwise in order to remove the belt.

c. Remove the belt.

d. Install a new belt.

e. Rotate the belt tensioner clockwise in order to install the belt.

f. Install the upper fan guard.

g. Lower the engine hood and latch the engine hood.

Figure 9-2　Fan Guard

# Practical Reading

## Air Conditioner/Cab Heater Filter(Recirculation)-Inspect/Replace

## 空气循环过滤芯——检查/更换

**Notice**

An air recirculation filter element plugged with dust will result in decreased performance and service life to the air conditioner or cab heater.①

To prevent decreased performance, clean the filter element, as required.

The air conditioner filter is located on the lower left side of the cab behind the seat(shown as Figure 9-3).

Inspeet/Replace steps:

1) Slide the operator seat forward.

2) Slide the filter element upward.

3) Tap the air filter in order to remove the dirt. Do not use compressed air to clean the filter.

4) After you clean the filter element, inspect the filter element. If the filter element is damaged

or badly contaminated, use a new filter element. Make sure that the filter element is dry.

5) Install the filter element.

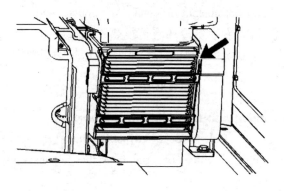

Figure 9-3　There is the Air Conditioner Filter

## Word List

1. slide[slaid]　　　　　　　　vt. 滑动；使滑动
2. dirt[də:t]　　　　　　　　　n. 污垢，泥土；灰尘，尘土
3. tap[tæp]　　　　　　　　　vt. 轻敲；轻打
4. contaminated[kən'tæmənetid]　adj. 受污染的；弄脏的

## Proper Names

1. filter element　　　　　　　滤芯
2. plugged with　　　　　　　被…堵上
3. result in　　　　　　　　　导致
4. service life　　　　　　　　使用寿命；使用期限
5. located on　　　　　　　　位于

## Notes

①An air recirculation filter element plugged with dust will result in decreased performance and service life to the air conditioner or cab heater.

空气循环过滤芯被尘土堵塞的话将会导致空调设备或空气加热设备性能和使用寿命的下降。

# 参考答案

**Read the following content and translate into chinese：**
皮带的检查、调整与更换
注：这台发动机装有皮带张紧装置，能够自动调节皮带的张紧力。
1) 拧松发动机罩并升高发动机罩；
2) 检查皮带是否磨损或者断裂；
3) 如果皮带需要更换的，则按照以下步骤进行：

a. 拆除上方的风扇罩(见图9-2);
b. 顺时针转动张紧器以便卸下皮带;
c. 拆除旧皮带;
d. 装上一个新皮带;
e. 再顺时针转动张紧器以便安装新皮带;
f. 装上上方的风扇罩;
g. 降下并拧紧发动机罩。

# 项目 10

# 动态仿真技术在工程机械设计上的应用

## 学习目标

完成本项目学习任务后,你应当能:

1. 了解动态仿真技术的发展情况,动态仿真技术的具体应用;掌握与设计相关的专业术语,了解工程机械设计的前沿动态;

2. 基于所学专业知识,借助专业词典能无障碍地查阅与机械设备设计方面的英语资料。

## 任务描述

以动态仿真技术在装载机上的设计为例,完成相关单词、词汇、特殊语句的学习。对工程机械动态仿真技术的背景等方面有一定的认识。强化相关专业英文资料的阅读能力。

## 引导问题

说说你所知道的基于计算机的机械设计技术或者软件有哪些?

## 学　时

2 学时

## 学习引导

本学习任务沿着以下脉络进行学习:

复习相关专业知识 → 学习单词和语法 → 通读全文 → 完成课后练习 → 课后阅读

# Project 10  Using Dynamic Simulation in the Development of Construction Machinery

As in the car industry for quite some time, dynamic simulation of complete vehicles is being practiced more and more in the development of off-road machinery. However, specific questions arise due not only to company structure and size, but especially to the type of product. Tightly coupled, non-linear subsystems of different domains make prediction and optimization of the complete system's dynamic behaviors a challenge. Furthermore, the demand for versatile machines leads to sometimes contradictory target requirements and can turn the design process into a hunt for the least painful compromise. This can be avoided by profound system knowledge, assisted by simulation driven product development. This paper gives an overview of joint research into this issue by Volvo Wheel Loaders and Linkoping University on that matter, and lists the results of a related literature review. Rather than giving detailed answers, the problem space for ongoing and future research is examined and possible solutions are sketched.

The general motives for "Virtual Prototyping" are probably familiar to all engineers: Stricter legal requirements (e.g. with regard to exhaust emissions and sound) and tougher customer demands (e.g. with regard to performance and handling) lead to more advanced, complex systems, which are harder to optimize. With traditional methods, development will cost more and need more time. In contrast to this, increased competition demands lower development cost and shorter project times.

"Virtual Prototyping" has been generally adopted in the vehicle industry as a major step towards solving this conflict both on the consumer side (cars) and on the commercial side (trucks and buses). Having started with simulation of sub-systems, the state-of-the-art is simulation of complete vehicles, mostly for evaluation of handling, comfort, and durability but also for crash-tests.

One reason for the off-road equipment industry lagging behind can be found in the size of these companies: being significantly smaller, broad investments in the latest CAE tools (together with the necessary training) take longer until amortisation. The other, and probably more important reason is that the products are very different to those of the on-road vehicle industry-not only geometrically (size), but topologically (sub-systems of various domains and their interconnections).

Cases have recently been published where complete machines were simulated for evaluation of the simulation technique itself, sub-systems, comfort-related aspects, or durability. This paper, will also deal with dynamic simulation of complete machines, but for analysis and optimization of overall performance and related aspects. The focus will be on wheel loaders with hydrodynamic transmissions, but most findings (and questions) will be also applicable to other off-road machinery.

Due to the versatility of these machines, wheel loaders need to fulfill a great many requirements, which are often interconnected and sometimes contradict each other. [1]This is true of essentially all industrial products and is widely recognized. Since this paper focuses on aspects of performance, other aspects such as total cost of ownership, market availability, reliability etc. will not be discussed explicitly.

To give just a few examples, the following performance-related aspects are important (varying with the working task):

1) Geometric parameters (lift height, digging depth, dump reach, parallel alignment).
2) Loads, torques and forces (tipping load, break-out torque, lift force, traction force).
3) Speeds and cycle times (complete machine and sub-systems).
4) Consumption and emissions (fuel consumption, exhaust emissions, sound & vibration).
5) Controllability (precision, feedback, response).

While some of the items are clearly determined by more than just one sub-system (e. g. lift force, which is determined by hydraulics and load unit), others seem to be possible to attribute to one single sub-system (e. g. traction force). One might thus wrongly be tempted to leave such aspects out of the optimization loop when it comes to trading-off product targets against each other when choosing technical solutions.

A modern wheel loader of hydro-dynamic design, however, consists of tightly coupled, non-linear sub-systems of different domains. Since all sub-systems interact even in seemingly simple cases, prediction and optimization of the complete system's dynamic behavior is a challenge. [2]

Figure 10-1 shows how the sub-systems of main interest are interacting when loading gravel.

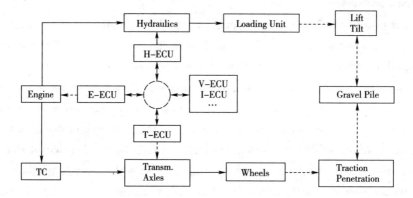

Figure10-1 Simplified transfer scheme of a wheel loader, loading gravel
(TC = Torque Converter, ECU = Electronic Control Unit, V = Vehicle, I = Instrument)

For loading granular material like gravel, the bucket first has to penetrate the pile. This requires traction force, which is achieved by transferring torque from the engine via a torque converter, transmission, axles, and wheels to the ground. A typical sequence for actually filling the bucket is then to break material by tilting backwards a little, lifting a little, and penetrating even further. The lift and tilt functions require engine torque to be transferred via hydraulic pumps (converting torque to hydraulic pressure), cylinders (converting hydraulic pressure to longitudinal force), and loading unit.

As shown, the two different transfer paths are competing for the limited engine torque. Furthermore, in the act of loading, these two paths are brought together in the gravel pile: the penetration establishes a reaction force at the bucket, which counteracts the break-out force, as well as the lift force. Like a short circuit, loads can be transferred back to the origin, in this case the engine, and lead to overload (greater interaction between the systems or the engine stops completely).

This has to be avoided by a design that carefully balances traction and lift/tilt. But these functions can not be optimized without influencing others, e.g. machine velocity and lifting time. In addition to this, Figure 10-1 neglects the fact that loading unit geometry and bucket design are of great importance for a smooth bucket filling. In addition, a machine operator who handles a loader in an unintelligent way can have difficulty in achieving a favorable balance. In such cases (but not exclusively), implementing sophisticated electronic control strategies can be of great help.

Above, one single phase in one single (yet frequent) handling case has been described. A typical loading cycle consists of several phases, where balance has to be established in each. Additionally, there are many different handling cases, each with its own requirements, which need to be satisfied.

With the ambition of developing a product that is significantly better than its predecessor every time, this becomes harder and harder to achieve. The trend towards more electronic control is as striking in the off-road equipment industry as it is in the on-road branch (passenger cars, trucks, and busses). In figure 10-1, this is symbolised by 5 electronic control units, each serving a specific purpose (component or sub-system). The ring represents the common data bus (CAN-bus) the ECU's are connected to.

## Word List

1. arise [ə'raiz]              vi. 出现;上升
2. domains [do'men]            n. 域,域名;领域;网域
3. optimization [ˌɔptimai'zeiʃənˌ]   n. 最佳化,最优化
4. painful ['penfl]            adj. 痛苦的;疼痛的
5. versatility [ˌvəsə'tiləti]   n. 多功能性;多才多艺

## Proper Names

1. dynamic simulation          动态仿真
2. off-road machinery          越野机械
3. Wheel Loaders               轮式装载机

## Notes

①Due to the versatility of these machines, wheel loaders need to fulfil a great many requirements, which are often interconnected and sometimes contradict each other.

由于这些机器的多功能性,装载机需要满足许多需求,这些需求通常是相互联系的,有时相互矛盾。

②A modern wheel loader of hydro-dynamic design, however, consists of tightly coupled, non-linear sub-systems of different domains. Since all sub-systems interact even in seemingly simple cases, prediction and optimisation of the complete system's dynamic behaviour is a challenge.

然而,一个现代轮式装载机的动态设计,包括紧密耦合、非线性子系统的不同领域。由于所有子系统即使似在简单的情况下交汇,对完整的系统的动态行为的预测和优化都是一个挑战。

# Practical Reading

## Computer-Integrated Manufacturing
## 计算机集成制造

Computer-Integrated Manufacturing(CIM) is the integration of the total manufacturing enterprise through the use of integrated systems and data communications coupled with new managerial philosophies that improve organizational and personnel efficiency.

CIM describes a new approach to manufacturing, management, and corporate operation. Although CIM systems can include many advanced manufacturing technologies such as robotics, Computer Numerical Control(CNC), Computer-Aided Design (CAD), Computer-Aided Manufacturing(CAM), Computer-Aided Engineering(CAE), and Just-In-Time(JIT) production, it goes beyond these technologies.①

CIM is a new way to do business that includes a commitment to total enterprise quality, continuous improvement, customer satisfaction, use of a single computer database for all product information that is the basis for manufacturing and production decisions in every department, removal of communication barriers among all departments, and the integration of enterprise resources.②

## Word List

1. integrated ['intigretid]          adj. 集成化的
2. commitment [kə'mitm(ə)nt]         n. 承担,付出

## Proper Names

1. Computer-Integrated Manufacturing (CIM)    计算机集成制造
2. coupled with                               …,再加上…
3. managerial philosophies                    管理体系
4. advanced manufacturing technologies        先进的制造技术
5. Computer-Aided Engineering(CAE)            计算机辅助工程
6. Just-In-Time(JIT)                          准时制生产

## Notes

①Although CIM systems can include many advanced manufacturing technologies such as robotics, Computer Numerical Control(CNC), Computer-Aided Design (CAD), Computer-Aided Manufacturing(CAM), Computer-Aided Engineering(CAE), and Just-In-Time (JIT) production, it goes beyond these technologies.

尽管计算机集成制造系统中可能包含有许多先进的制造技术,例如:机器人、数控、计算机辅助设计、计算机辅助制造、计算机辅助工程和准时制生产等,但它超越了这些技术。

语句 Although CIM systems can include many advanced manufacturing technologies such as robotics…为让步状语从句。主句中 it 指代 CIM systems。

②CIM is a new way to do business that includes a commitment to total enterprise quality, continuous improvement, customer satisfaction, use of a single computer database for all product information that is the basis for manufacturing and production decisions in every department, removal of communication barriers among all departments, and the integration of enterprise resources.

  计算机集成制造是一种新的包含一揽子事务的处理方式,这些事务包括整个企业性能、连续的改进性、客户的满意性,以及一个单独的计算机数据库的使用。该数据库用于处理全部生产信息,其基本内容是每个部门中对于制造和生产的决定、所有的部门中通信障碍的排除、企业资源的综合安排。本语句采用的是正式定义的语句的写作方式。

# 参 考 文 献

[1] 宋永刚. 工程机械专业英语[M]. 北京:人民交通出版社,2006.
[2] 杨承先. 现代工程建设机械专业英语[M]. 北京:人民交通出版社,2009.
[3] 李美荣. 工程机械专业英语[M]. 北京:人民交通出版社,2008.
[4] Jan-Ove Palmberg. Fluid and Mechanical Engineering Systems. Department of Mechanical Engineering. Linköping University. S-581 83. Linköping. Sweden. Proceedings of The Eighth Scandinavian International Conference on Fluid Power, SICFP'03, May 7-9,2003,Tampere, Finland.
[5] http://en.wikipedia.org/wiki/Main_Page.